SCHEDULING FOR

PERSONALIZED
COMPETENCY-BASED
EDUCATION

Douglas **FINN III**   Michelle **FINN**

MARZANO
Resources

555 North Morton Street
Bloomington, IN 47404
888.849.0851
FAX: 866.801.1447

email: info@MarzanoResources.com
MarzanoResources.com

Printed in the United States of America

Library of Congress Cataloging-in-Publication Data

Names: Finn, Douglas E., III, author. | Finn, Michelle, author.
Title: Scheduling for personalized competency-based education / Douglas E.
    Finn III and Michelle M. Finn.
Description: Bloomington, IN : Marzano Resources, 2020. | Includes
    bibliographical references and index.
Identifiers: LCCN 2020038751 (print) | LCCN 2020038752 (ebook) | ISBN
    9781943360314 (paperback) | ISBN 9781943360321 (ebook)
Subjects: LCSH: Competency-based education. | Individualized instruction.
Classification: LCC LC1031 .F46 2020 (print) | LCC LC1031 (ebook) | DDC
    379.1/55--dc23
LC record available at https://lccn.loc.gov/2020038751
LC ebook record available at https://lccn.loc.gov/2020038752

Production Team

President and Publisher: Douglas M. Rife
Associate Publisher: Sarah Payne-Mills
Art Director: Rian Anderson
Managing Production Editor: Kendra Slayton
Production Editor: Laurel Hecker
Content Development Specialist: Amy Rubenstein
Copy Editor: Jessi Finn
Editorial Assistants: Sarah Ludwig and Elijah Oates

To Rick H. Thank you for all the late-night conversations.

—D. F.

To all those dedicated educators out there, for whom the status quo has never been enough. Thank you for what you do each and every day to better the lives of children.

—M. F.

Acknowledgments

The authors would like to thank the following contributors from the leadership team of Benson Middle School in Benson, North Carolina, for their instrumental work in PCBE and their willingness to share their insights and examples of the scheduling process:

Dana Jernigan, Principal

Pamela Routhier, Assistant Principal

Jeffery Henry, Assistant Principal

The authors would like to thank Pamela Swanson, Superintendent of Schools in Westminster Public Schools, and the following contributors from the district leadership team for their instrumental work in PCBE and their willingness to share their insights and examples of the scheduling process:

Oliver Grenham, Chief Education Officer

Jeni Gotto, Executive Director of Teaching & Learning

Amber Swieckowski, Principal, Hodgkins Leadership Academy

Roger Vadeen, Principal, Sunset Ridge Elementary School

Peter Rainey, Assistant Principal, Westminster High School

The authors would also like to acknowledge the instrumental early work of the Chugach School District, Bering Strait School District, and Reinventing Schools Coalition for being pioneers of the PCBE movement and for making them the educators they are today.

Marzano Resources would like to thank the following reviewers:

Chris Garcia
Principal
Severance High School
Severance, Colorado

Eleanor B. Patrick
Principal
Oak Road Academy
New Bern, North Carolina

Shanna Martin
Social Studies and Technology Teacher
Instructional Coach
Lomira Middle School
Lomira, Wisconsin

Mona Yanacheak
Education Consultant
Northwest Area Education Agency
Sioux City, Iowa

Table of Contents

Chapter 3
An Overview of PCBE Scheduling **51**

Chapter 4
Creation of a Horizontal PCBE Schedule **67**

Chapter 5
Creation of a Vertical PCBE Schedule 83

Chapter 6
PCBE Implementation Within Stand-Alone Classrooms. 99

Appendix
Example PCBE Schedules. 125

About the Authors

Douglas Finn III is a leading educator in personalized competency-based education (PCBE) and has worked in the area of PCBE since 2004. Within PCBE, he has taught every grade level, from primary school through graduation, and has been an instructional and administrative coach for schools, districts, and state departments throughout the United States and the world. He prides himself on having practical application knowledge for implementing PCBE at all levels. Doug has supported the transition to PCBE as a professional development associate since 2008, first for the nonprofit Re-Inventing Schools Coalition (RISC) and now for Marzano Resources. Doug is also an implementation lead for the nonprofit Marzano Academies. He is a coauthor of *A Handbook for Personalized Competency-Based Education* with Robert J. Marzano, Jennifer S. Norford, and Michelle Finn. He received a bachelor's degree in geology from the University of Montana.

Michelle Finn is a professional development associate with Marzano Resources and implementation lead for Marzano Academies, a nonprofit that provides schools a comprehensive, long-term approach to implementing research-based practices within PCBE. Since 2004, she has worked on the implementation and support of PCBE in schools and districts around the United States. During her career, she has taught at all grade levels from kindergarten to tenth grade. Her particular passion is building student agency through learning transparency, goal setting, voice, and choice. Michelle coauthored *A Handbook for Personalized Competency-Based Education* with Robert J. Marzano, Jennifer S. Norford, and Douglas Finn III. She graduated with a bachelor of science in elementary education from the University of Maine and a master's degree in educational leadership from Saint Joseph's College.

To book Douglas Finn III or Michelle Finn for professional development, contact pd@MarzanoResources.com.

Introduction

The Transition to Personalized Competency-Based Education

Personalized competency-based education (PCBE) is a model of schooling that blends the tenets of competency-based education and personalized learning. The characteristics of PCBE, as defined in *A Handbook for Personalized Competency-Based Education*, are as follows:

- Students move on to the next level within a subject area only after they have demonstrated proficiency at the current level.

- Students learn content at their own pace, so time is not a factor in judging their competencies.

- Students have multiple opportunities and ways to learn specific content.

- Students have multiple opportunities and ways to demonstrate proficiency with specific content.

- Students develop agency (a central focus, in addition to proficiency with academic content).

- Students have a voice in the teaching and learning process.

- Students have choices in the teaching and learning process. (Marzano, Norford, Finn, & Finn, 2017, p. 6)

As the preceding list outlines, PCBE is rooted in a reimagination of the traditional educational grouping and pacing framework. Traditionally, districts and schools group students into age-based classrooms called *grades*. These students move on from their grade's content requirements on a yearly school schedule, regardless (in most cases) of their academic proficiency on the grade-level expectations. PCBE shifts the focus from an education schedule in which *time* determines how a student moves through the grade levels to one in which the student's *acquired learning* becomes the determining factor for progress. Thus, schools need to design schedules that support such a system of flexibly paced, mastery-based learning.

Why This Book Is Needed

When Robert J. Marzano and Jennifer S. Norford invited us to coauthor *A Handbook for Personalized Competency-Based Education* (Marzano et al., 2017), we understood that some aspects of the PCBE approach might need additional detail and clarification beyond what we could present in the handbook. In our work with districts all over the United States as they explore and implement the PCBE approach, we are continually asked to help organize students' movement through the scope and sequence of learning expectations—that is, districts seek help with scheduling. This book expands on the handbook's chapter on scheduling to better assist schools and districts in this transition.

We recommend that readers seeking a full overview of all the components of PCBE read *A Handbook for Personalized Competency-Based Education* (Marzano et al., 2017) before reading this book. This book is set up to give readers a brief background understanding of PCBE, but it does not share a complete discussion of all aspects of this approach. The PCBE definitions and model are consistent between this book and the handbook.

Support for many aspects of PCBE has been growing since the early 2000s, as school districts have moved toward state, provincial, or national content standards; more accurate and reliable grading practices; and student-centered approaches to teaching and learning. But the foundational components and mindset changes required by a shift from traditional educational systems to PCBE systems create a variety of sticking points. A challenge at the heart of PCBE is grouping and scheduling students according to their learning needs rather than their age. Schools trying to shift to a PCBE model often miss the elements of flexible pacing and the scope and sequence of learning that PCBE requires. Many schools instead try to personalize standards-based instruction within an age-based classroom. This, in turn, creates an unsustainable structure for educators: it requires them to address all students' individual zones of proximal development, which, within an age-based classroom, involves a wide span of academic content. Though it is more targeted in terms of individual instruction, this partial implementation creates the same types of gaps that are so difficult to address in traditional classrooms.

The professional literature on PCBE has not previously provided a deep dive into the foundational components of grouping and scheduling students as they move through a PCBE system. This has left educators to attempt the transition with little guidance. Without clear guidelines for how to effectively schedule learning, most schools and districts attempting this transition have gotten stuck in both worlds, essentially straddling the divide between the traditional system and the PCBE system, two frameworks that are neither fully compatible nor easily overlaid. With this book, we seek to deepen understanding of PCBE scheduling so school leaders and educators may develop systems to fully integrate all the aspects of PCBE within their classrooms, schools, and districts.

How This Book Is Organized

The first chapter of this book gives an overview of the challenges of the traditional educational system and the reasons for shifting to a PCBE system. Again, this book provides only a brief review of the aspects of PCBE other than scheduling. Readers should consult *A Handbook for Personalized Competency-Based Education* (Marzano et al., 2017) to establish a comprehensive understanding of this model.

Chapter 2 describes a very important part of beginning the PCBE scheduling process: understanding the different sets of student data needed to successfully implement a PCBE schedule. Because information about individual students and their learning relative to standards drives the decisions within a PCBE system, gathering standards-based data and analyzing them are foundational components of scheduling. PCBE scheduling relies on two sets of student data: (1) grade-level data, which support schools' broader grouping of students into classes, and (2) specific standards data, which support the placement of individual students within each of the classes. Both are used in conjunction to develop the most accurate PCBE schedule. These areas are critical to the success of implementing a PCBE system, as creating a schoolwide schedule and assigning students to groups and classes within it require that schools accurately gather and utilize these data. To illustrate these concepts, we introduce a sample school and mock data that will appear throughout the remaining chapters.

Chapter 3 gives an overview of a PCBE approach to scheduling, introducing the concepts that underpin both horizontal and vertical scheduling options. This chapter further discusses placement strategies for grouping students, including fine-tuning and reorganizing groups based on student needs. Knowing the inherent challenges before undertaking these large-scale transitions is important.

Chapter 4 explores horizontal PCBE schedules in depth; chapter 5 does the same for vertical PCBE schedules. These chapters provide educators and administrators with greater clarity on designing and implementing each scheduling option. The detailed information will assist them with deciding which option is better for a specific school site.

Chapter 6 features ideas of how to enact some aspects of PCBE scheduling within a single classroom setting. These ideas will benefit individual teachers who are interested in PCBE but who work in schools that are not necessarily implementing all or part of this framework.

Finally, the book ends with an appendix that provides extended examples of PCBE school schedules. Throughout the book, we use the terms *teacher* and *educator* to signify any individual who instructs, assesses, or supports students in their academic needs. The terms *scheduling team* and *schedulers* denote anyone involved in the scheduling process. This may and should include teachers, special education staff, support staff, administrators, and district office staff. Scheduling teams may also be broken up into smaller subgroups for efficiency and more targeted decision making for subgroups of the student population.

With a full transition to PCBE, students progress through school based on their learning—not based on the simple passage of time. This certainly benefits the students, but it benefits the teachers as well because they do not have to meet the myriad of student learning needs in an age-based classroom. The PCBE model is at its core a student-centered model. But because educators are the ones who make learning happen for young people day after day, the success of PCBE, like any initiative or system change, hinges not only on teacher understanding and buy-in but also on sustainability of practice. For these critical reasons, we recommend a transition to *all* aspects of PCBE—including grouping students according to their learning needs and creating a schoolwide schedule to match. This book provides the necessary information to assist schools in doing just that.

Chapter 1

Differences Between Traditional Education Systems and PCBE Systems

It's important for us to know ourselves and how we're doing so when we grow up, we will know what we're good at and how to get better at things.

—Fourth-grade student

Across section of students in any classroom operating under traditional, age-based groupings will reflect an enormous range of knowledge and ability. The students' proficiency levels are nearly always spread out across several years of grade-level content. For example, an age-based fourth-grade classroom might include students who read at levels ranging from second grade to seventh grade. With this wide variation comes significant problems inherent in age-based groupings in terms of instruction and, at times, behavior. Students who already know the grade level's content are not allowed to move on, and students who cannot learn all the content in the set time are forced to either move on and accumulate learning gaps or redo that grade level's entire scope of learning as if they had not mastered anything at all. This is fundamentally inefficient and unfair to both students and the teachers who are trying to meet the large spread of needs within their age-based classrooms.

Imagine telling a student that she has to learn to swim in the months of September and October. At the end of October, the term for learning to swim will close. Swim lessons, opportunities to practice, and opportunities to show progress will cease, and you will generate a report. If the student does not succeed in time, you will record her as failing to swim—regardless of whether she learns the skill at a later time. Even worse, the student must move into advanced swim lessons in November and December, where her swim instructor expects her to perform more complex skills, such as the butterfly and the breaststroke—even though she hasn't yet mastered the foundations of how to kick and breathe and float. It's no surprise that students fall further and further behind as their learning gaps compound.

PCBE takes a different approach. It puts an emphasis on equity and provides opportunities for *all* students to master the scope and sequence of content, regardless of the amount of time they require to obtain mastery. It places value on the learning itself rather than on time; the outcome is most students graduate with a full set of knowledge and skills, rather than just a handful of students reaching that level while the remainder leave the school system with an incomplete set.

PCBE allows students opportunities to freely move through the curriculum content at their pace, not the district- or teacher-determined pace. Students who need more time are no longer left behind. Fast-paced students are no longer held back. The core of the content standards is guaranteed for all students, but fast-paced students might gain added opportunities, such as advanced placement for college credits, internships, and early graduation, and slower-paced students might be given additional time for graduation, internships, or flexibility of schedule for a work-school environment that best meets their needs. Standards-based grading practices (a key aspect of PCBE) are based on a scale of 1 to 4, where 3 denotes proficiency. This gives students the ability to go above and beyond on required standards, earning a 4, which denotes advanced thinking or additional levels of complexity.

Some skeptics might argue that allowing students additional time and opportunities to show what they know is unfair—that doing so is "not like the real world." They might argue that it is unfair to students who can master the concepts at the predetermined pace. Students who are succeeding in the traditional system (or, more likely, their parents) may like the acknowledgment that comes from ranking students. We maintain that learning is not a race and that, in fact, PCBE is much *more* in keeping with the real world than the traditional educational system. When people fail a driver's test, for example, they receive additional time and attempts at mastery. They are also not penalized or stigmatized in any way, aside from perhaps a little teasing from their friends. No mark on a car or license stigmatizes a driver for not passing the first attempt. Also, no sign applauds a driver for passing the test the first time. People can also take multiple attempts on other high-stakes tests, such as the bar exam. In the real world, there is job training to hone skills, and differences in learning speed and preference are generally accepted as normal. Thus, it is the traditional educational system that is at odds with the real world.

PCBE can solve problems inherent to the traditional system, but it necessitates a fundamental change not just in practice but also in mindset. It requires that educators help students shift their thinking away from comparing themselves to others and toward considering their growth from their previous selves to their current and future selves. Educators and parents must adopt this growth mindset as well. Instead of asking how much better or worse they are at a skill compared to another student, students should have a more personal, goal-oriented mindset. They can apply this kind of mindset by asking questions like the following.

- "How much have I improved in this area?"
- "What do I need to do to get better?"
- "What do my data tell me?"
- "What strategies worked best for me when I was learning this skill, and why?"
- "What is my next step in this learning, and how am I going to get there?"

To provide context for this new mindset, this chapter will provide a brief overview of the components and desired outcomes of PCBE, concerns for the transition process, and the foundation of PCBE scheduling.

Components and Desired Outcomes of PCBE

As mentioned in the introduction (page 1), PCBE consists of several essential components. It is certainly helpful to understand each component individually, but just as important to understand how each component connects with the others to form a framework. The components are meant to work as interrelated parts of a whole rather than as stand-alone pieces. Think of PCBE as a modern house with a common set of systems. In order to be a fully functioning, effective structure, the house needs electrical, plumbing, and HVAC systems embedded within structural components such as walls, a roof, floors, entry and exit points, windows, and a foundation. All these components work together to create the most livable structure. If one component is left unfinished, the house will not be livable. For instance, if the house's electrical system is not hooked up to the power grid, then the HVAC system won't work, and neither will parts of the plumbing system that rely on electricity. If no foundation is built, the walls will buckle and twist under the house's unsupported weight, impacting the structural integrity as a whole.

We do not use this analogy lightly. One of the reasons to shift to PCBE is to make students feel more "at home" in educational spaces and make the learning itself more personalized to the individual. Thus, creating the PCBE house means ensuring that all the relevant components are in place and fully integrated. The four components we note here are (1) developing standards and scoring consistency, (2) gathering standards-based student data, (3) establishing personalized instruction, and (4) developing student agency. For more information on each topic, please consult *A Handbook for Personalized Competency-Based Education* (Marzano et al., 2017).

Developing Standards and Scoring Consistency

When you build a new house, you first have to clear and level the land you're going to build on. Prior to a full shift to PCBE, the equivalent step is to identify a scope and sequence of standards and create systemwide scoring procedures. In other words, the curriculum for each content area and grade level must be defined as a manageable set of standards, and teachers must use a consistent method to score student learning against those standards. Marzano and colleagues (2017) also recommend implementing a standards-based grading system with proficiency scales to increase reliability. This shift in grading practices may happen as a slow transition over several years to support teachers' developing knowledge and allow current students to phase into new expectations and a new reporting system.

With a scope and sequence of standards in place, as well as common scoring practices to ensure inter-rater reliability, the groundwork is laid to allow students to move more freely through the learning expectations.

Gathering Standards-Based Student Data

The next critical step is to gather standards-based student data. Too often, schools attempt to jump into grouping and regrouping students without acquiring accurate standards-based data—which we might compare to building a house directly on the cleared ground without pouring a foundation to support the structure. Student data act as the foundation of PCBE because they clarify what students know currently and what they need to learn within the scope and sequence of expectations. That clarity shifts the foundations of scheduling from age-based criteria to a new set of need-based criteria that is truly responsive to individual students. Without standards-based student data there is no starting point or reference with which to align instruction to student need. The importance of collecting accurate data on student proficiency across all standards in all content areas cannot be emphasized enough; this information is crucial to the PCBE structure. Without these data underpinning the transition to PCBE, the same issues that come with age-based grouping will surface.

Establishing Personalized Instruction

A PCBE system offers multiple pathways to proficiency, in recognition that no two students learn in exactly the same way. It thus moves instruction and assessment of content-area standards from a one-size-fits-all approach to an approach that allows students to learn and show content mastery in various ways. As students progress through the content, they have access to multiple opportunities to learn and prove mastery of the content. This is not to say that all students necessarily get individualized instruction on every standard or have their own specialized assessments on every skill; it means that more than one type of instruction and assessment is available on every standard for every student. This honors the students' widely diverse interests and learning preferences and prioritizes proficiency rather than time.

Differentiating instruction is not a novel concept, but it is one that teachers find difficult to fully integrate in traditional classrooms because they must attempt to administer strategies and content for a wide range of readiness levels. The Nation's Report Card (2019) found that less than half of students tested were at or above proficiency, ranging from as low as 25 percent proficient to as high as 41 percent proficient, on the National Assessment of Educational Progress for mathematics and reading in grades 4, 8, and 12. Is it any wonder that well-meaning educators are forced to spend critical time addressing below-grade-level content to prepare many students for the required age-based content? On the other side of the coin, many district- and curriculum-mandated pacing guides allow little flexibility or time to move outside the grade-level expectations, so teachers are not able to fill learning gaps that they encounter, those gaps compound, and students move ahead even farther from proficiency on grade-level expectations.

Personalization of instruction, assessment, and the environment can then incorporate subtler areas such as student interests and strengths, which can lead to more meaningful learning, increased engagement, and stronger motivation. This approach offers students who, for example, have high content-area knowledge in science but aren't as strong with writing additional ways to show what they know. It also supports individuals' learning preferences, which may increase interest and hence motivation, though it may or may not be as instrumental to increased learning or retention (Brown, Roediger, & McDaniel, 2014). Personalization also creates more interweaving of modalities such as Richard E. Mayer's (2009) *Multimedia Learning*, which, for example, might pair auditory description with visual cues to deepen understanding and retention. No matter the student, learning or practicing in just one way is not as effective as a mixed approach that incorporates both a variety of modalities and spacing between practice (Brown et al., 2014). Multimodal instruction also supports students who might have cognitive difficulties such as auditory processing disorder, for example, by ensuring they receive information and practice skills in more ways than just lectures or discussion. Many students with such learning needs may have individualized education plans (IEPs), which ensure they have supports in place, but many students do not have such supports and could benefit from these changes in standard practice.

Personalization also allows the individual educators to leverage their own interests and strengths into giving students additional ways to learn. For example, an educator who has a particular skill in coding might offer instruction, practice, or assessment through gaming or app development. Perhaps an educator who has a connection to a local farm could utilize it for a cross-curricular, hands-on science or social studies unit. The possibilities are endless and allow educators to delve into their passions and unlock the art of teaching.

Developing Student Agency

The components of developing student agency and offering voice and choice can work in tandem to build students' self-efficacy, which "involves the belief that one is ultimately in control of one's own life and the development of the accompanying skills to actualize this belief" (Marzano et al., 2017, p. 37). These components emphasize including students in the learning process and in learning decisions, fostering their ability to actively shape their learning experience and shifting control from a purely teacher-centered model to a more student-centered one.

These components must develop over time; teachers should take care to avoid offering new voice and choice opportunities before students have developed enough agency to effectively manage them. Just as academic readiness is a key factor in students' success with content-area expectations, the development of student agency is a key factor in the success of implementing highly flexible learning options.

What we find, when speaking with students at all grade levels in schools implementing tenets of PCBE, is that when students and educators are motivated to take an active role, they usually see a positive change in themselves. During a conversation with a fourth grader in 2014, for example, he stated, "I like being able to use my freedom of speech and get a say in what we do. The teacher might even change things that we didn't like or that weren't working for us, and it makes me feel really good to be listened to." This inclusion builds self-efficacy over time as students begin to see how their ideas lead to changes in the classroom and they become more involved in every aspect of school from the environment, to the culture, to the learning itself.

Educators see the change in students as well and this inspires them and builds their own motivation and passion, as fourth-grade teacher Christine Palmer remarked:

> When I first heard about this initiative, it was really scary because it was very different than what I had been doing in the last few years, although I knew in my heart it would be best for the kids. . . . The biggest change I'm seeing is they are really starting to own their own learning and to me that's a lesson that they need for life. So, no matter what the standards are, no matter what their goal is, if they're leading their own learning, then in fact I feel that that's a triumph. (personal communication, November 6, 2014)

Caitlin Gerrity, a media center specialist, put it this way:

> It has completely transformed the way my classroom operates. It has changed my belief system in allowing freedom to not be a scary thing in the classroom because I sort of felt that once they're not all on the carpet in front of my SMART Board, it would be chaotic. But in fact, it has completely transformed the way behavior management happens in my classroom and allowing students to have that freedom of choice and responsibility for their own learning has ignited their interest in learning in a way I could have never expected. (personal communication, March 11, 2015)

Educators also mention additional support and connection. Jessica Collins remarked about her experiences with PCBE this way: "I do feel supported in what I do, and I can talk to other people and the collaboration that I have now . . . I love sharing what I do" (personal communication, March 9, 2015).

When students feel like valued classroom citizens, their confidence and ability to make effective choices rise, no matter their age. When talking about voice and choice in learning, one four-year-old preschooler in a PCBE pilot classroom joyously exclaimed in 2014, "We do it our own self and we're kids, and we can do it!"

The Transition to PCBE

PCBE is the kind of "deep change" that Robert J. Marzano, Timothy Waters, and Brian A. McNulty (2005) said "alters the system in fundamental ways" that require "new ways of thinking and acting" (p. 66). Change of this magnitude necessitates understanding and buy-in prior to implementation. The more that stakeholder groups understand and accept how the change to PCBE solves existing issues and benefits students, the better the chance that the new system will succeed in the long term.

PCBE is, at its core, about better meeting student needs, which is a powerful platform from which to build any new system.

If the magnitude of this change intimidates stakeholders, they may backpedal from the implementation goals and try to meld the school's existing framework with PCBE—that is, they may try to implement what's known as a *first-order change*, in which the existing structure remains intact but behaviors within that structure change. First-order changes do not disrupt existing paradigms, beliefs, or resources because they aren't major shifts from what is currently in place. However, PCBE is not a first-order change, where overlaying the old with the new is relatively easy. Implementation of a PCBE model significantly alters the current system and requires major shifts in structure, mindset, approach, and skills. PCBE is a *second-order change*—a change that represents a systemic shift from prior behavior (Solution Tree, 2009). For that reason, leadership, the inclusion of students and staff, and systemwide implementation are all important in transitioning a school or district to PCBE; we discuss these topics in the following sections.

The Importance of Leadership

Leadership is a critical factor to the success of any change, including the transition to PCBE; leadership must be in place prior to implementation to support this transition. According to Marzano and colleagues (2005), "The leadership supporting an innovation must be consistent with the order of magnitude of the change" (p. 66). Due to the complexity of this change to PCBE, a strong leader who is committed to this transition must lead it. This leadership may be the factor that determines the transition's success.

Strong PCBE leaders have certain qualities that set them apart in their ability to convey, implement, and manage the change, as well as to sustain the system long-term. They possess an ability to create and communicate the vision to stakeholders in such a way that is both purposeful and inspirational. This engenders critical initial buy-in, but it also permeates everything they do as leaders, continuously ensuring the alignment and actualization of those core tenets. PCBE leaders also possess a strong belief in shared leadership at all levels—from students, to parents, to community members, to staff. They support building the capacity of all stakeholders to create the newly envisioned system as a team, which is also reflected in their hiring and evaluation processes. Great leaders know that it shouldn't be about *them*, and they work to ensure the sustainability of PCBE long after they're gone. Lastly, their ability to implement a continuous improvement model of evaluation, reflection, and modification allows for positive growth and a goal-setting approach that can weather the many ups and downs inherent in educational environments.

Since classroom teachers are responsible for much of the implementation, it is critical that they are *all* supported in gaining capacity for implementation and share leadership of the transition to PCBE. Creating a culture of shared leadership, support, and two-way communication ensures that the transition is not about one person's ideas but a shared effort among staff, students, parents, and community members. Michael Fullan (2001) stated that "deep and sustained reform depends on many of us" (p. 2), so success over time depends on leaders' bringing stakeholder groups into this process early on so that they help craft the implementation goals.

The Importance of Student and Staff Inclusion

Stakeholders include the students themselves. The fact that they are children does not mean they should not have a say in what happens to them. Unfortunately, the traditional system gives students very little input. Schooling is often passive for students. They are told what, when, and how to do everything. This lack of autonomy can affect motivation and detach students from the learning process, making them passive recipients in their own classroom experiences. Ask any student what they are learning and why, and the most common answer within a traditional educational system is a shrug. Content may be too difficult for students, or at times too easy. Either experience can affect motivation. If the content is so challenging that students are lost, they will feel defeated before they even begin. If it is too easy, they lack the sense of accomplishment that comes from gaining new skills and knowledge.

The transition to PCBE is about creating better conditions for students to succeed in their learning and in life, and a key part of that is motivating students. Daniel H. Pink (2009) outlined three factors that help people feel motivated and do their best work: (1) autonomy, (2) mastery, and (3) purpose. In other words, these factors represent "our innate need to direct our own lives, to learn and create new things, and to do better by ourselves and our world" (Pink, 2009, p. 10). Children are people too, and they have the same kinds of needs as adults do when it comes to having a say in their lives.

PCBE addresses all three of Pink's (2009) factors by offering voice, choice, and goal setting to support student autonomy (or *self-efficacy*) and purpose, and a "Goldilocks" approach to mastery that offers learning within a student's zone of proximal development. Having voice and choice within the culture, environment, and learning process provides autonomy and actively engages students in every part of their educational experience. When it comes to purpose, educators should know what they are teaching and why, and should convey that clarity to their students (Hattie, 2018). Students within PCBE are shown the scope and sequence of learning expectations, set goals around their learning, and track their progress. When students understand the relevance of the learning expectations, there is a clear a purpose for gaining new knowledge and skills, contributing to motivation. Finally, in PCBE, grouping students based on standards-based data means that learning is at an appropriate challenge level where mastery is both achievable and stimulating. All three of Pink's factors—autonomy, purpose, and mastery—work in tandem to increase the chances of a successful and fulfilling educational experience for students.

During the transition itself, there should be an emphasis on gathering stakeholder voices, so leaders should develop feedback loops for students and staff to be able to communicate their ideas and feelings about decisions prior to the change process. Initially, it may be helpful to allow anonymity to ensure stakeholders feel comfortable sharing their thoughts and feelings. Working toward an open, trusting environment with a free flow of information should be a goal of the process, but not an initial assumption. Though the transition is guided by core tenets that create a framework of required components, there is ample room for input or changes within how, when, and to what degree those components are implemented, so stakeholders should be included in the decision-making process as much as possible.

For instance, standards-based design is a core component of PCBE, but there is much flexibility for teachers in how instruction might look in a classroom, or how implementation might be scaffolded across or within content areas and grade levels. Leaders should view their whole staff team as a problem-solving and idea-generating entity rather than a group that information and decisions eventually trickle down to. Obviously, not all decisions are something that requires input. Some core transitional decisions have to be made by smaller groups of people for efficiency and as a function of leadership—to guide others. Leaders create the framework within which shared decisions fill in the day-to-day workings of implementation. With this in mind, there should be clarity around this process and which stakeholders handle which levels and areas of decision making. It should be clear to staff where and how their input is needed and how it will be utilized. There should be strong protocols in place for input gathering to ensure the input is specific and civil. Whether it be during meetings, through digital means, or in a physical spot such as a box or board, staff should know how, when, and why input is gathered. Leadership should not ask for input into decisions if that input is not truly going to be used in the decision-making process.

Similarly, students should be part of the input and decision-making process as much as is feasible. This may happen on a schoolwide scale when it comes to something that all students have in common, such as lunch or hallway procedures. More often it will happen at the classroom level, with a differing level of input from class to class depending on where the teacher might place emphasis in the implementation of voice and choice. Some teachers may afford a lot of input into the physical environment whereas others may emphasize the flexibility of assessment options. Just as with staff, PCBE and the transition process should be transparent to the students, and, if helpful, input might be anonymous. Just as with staff, there should be strong protocols in place for input gathering to ensure the input is specific and civil. Students may need help building this skill initially, as giving focused feedback or input is not necessarily something they may be familiar with. If protocols are not followed, it can be a strong learning opportunity. For example, if there is a digital input board, a teacher may approve comments as students begin to learn how to give effective feedback. They might anonymously share a comment that did not follow the protocol as a teaching tool. Maybe the language was harsh or inappropriate, or it was vague or unrelated to the topic. The teacher could ask, "How might we make this better?" Thus, the teacher problem-solves with students rather than punishing a student who, for whatever reason, still has a long way to go toward offering effective input. Ideally, over time, this transparency allows for a safer environment where students feel their voices are both meaningful and valued. Just as with leadership and staff, teachers should not assume initially that the environment is such that all students feel safe and comfortable sharing their input, but that is ultimately what everyone should be steadily working toward: creating an environment of trust where every individual has agency to share and help change the school for the better.

The Importance of Systemwide Implementation

PCBE is best implemented across an entire school or system to avoid creating inconsistent expectations. When flexible scheduling is embedded systemwide, students are at their ideal zone of proximal development, rather than pushed ahead prematurely or held back unnecessarily.

If flexible pacing is developed within age-based classrooms, different classroom teachers may use differing levels of implementation, with some allowing for a high degree of flexibility and others offering little to no flexibility in movement through the standards. Students wind up getting what they need only by chance, depending on their teacher's ability to manage a large range of learning needs. Students who experience a high level of PCBE implementation end up feeling let down in successive years if they move to less flexible classrooms. When asked by his mother about this experience of moving from a PCBE classroom to a traditional one, a ten-year-old fourth grader put it this way:

> This year, it's more confusing than last year, because last year it was easier to understand. We had a matrix and it was just a lot easier because we had a learning target that we knew. Everyone was not on the same thing. People were on subtraction; they were on multiplication; some were on division; some were on geometry. This year, we're all in one big geometry group and some of the kids should still be on subtraction from last year! (K. Mathieu, personal communication, February 26, 2015)

When asked what he would change, this student was quick to say he would change everything back to the way it had been the previous year, where he tracked his own progress on his matrix and moved at a pace that was right for him. So, while it *is* possible to try to straddle both worlds and flexibly pace content within age-based classrooms, the results of this are often highly variable. Students' experience with PCBE should not be left up to the luck of the draw.

The Foundation of PCBE Scheduling

In *A Handbook for Personalized Competency-Based Education*, Marzano and colleagues (2017) outline seven design questions that form the framework for creating an effective PCBE system.

1. What content will we address?
2. How will the learning environment support student agency?
3. How will instruction support student learning?
4. How will teachers measure student proficiency?
5. How will scheduling accommodate student learning?

6. How will reporting facilitate student learning?

7. How do schools and districts transition to a PCBE system?

The fifth design question introduces the idea of scheduling students according to their learning needs. This aspect of PCBE systems is particularly important and the subject of this book because creating a PCBE schedule enhances the learning environment for both the students and educators by establishing classes based on the learning needs of the students. The classes focus on a narrower range of topics compared to an age-based classroom. This narrower range of content provides more opportunities for targeted instruction, assessment, and progress monitoring with students and decreases the preparation time when designing lessons and units.

Two approaches to scheduling are presented within *A Handbook for Personalized Competency-Based Education*: (1) tweaking a traditional schedule and (2) completely rethinking the scheduling process to create a more effective PCBE schedule (Marzano et al., 2017). The second option—completely rethinking the scheduling process for students based on their learning needs—is underutilized in PCBE implementation. The following sections illustrate how rethinking the scheduling process, organizing students based on their learning needs, and supporting students to move at an appropriate pace help make the foundation of PCBE as effective as possible.

Rethinking the Scheduling Process

It is understandable why schools do not rethink scheduling as much as they should in PCBE implementation. The shift from an age-based schedule to a student-needs-focused schedule involves using student data that schools do not normally incorporate to this extent in the scheduling process. Using such detailed student data as the starting point for a schedule can create a more complex scheduling process, which can look very intimidating at first.

Unfortunately, schools often respond to this challenge by implementing PCBE halfway—that is, they perform the needed data analysis but then assign the educators to age-based classes. As alluded to previously, this puts the educators *and* the students in a difficult situation, because the educators are expected to differentiate instruction for all their students, who all have different learning needs. In theory, this sounds great, but in practice, it can be overwhelming. This is where the statement, "I am teaching twenty students doing twenty different things," comes from. Differentiating instruction in an effort to meet the needs of all an age-based classroom's students can create an unsustainable workload for educators due to the range of needs in the class. When Janine M. Firmender, Sally M. Reis, and Sheelah M. Sweeny (2012) researched reading comprehension ranges within diverse classrooms, they found spreads of more than six grade levels in the third-grade classrooms that they studied, with the range growing ever wider each successive year. Based on this research, schools can conservatively estimate every age-based class has a minimum of a five-grade-level spread. Dealing with such a wide range of needs is unrealistic considering the time needed for preparation, instruction, and organization of how the students interact during the class period.

Now, compare that to what takes place within a school that has a PCBE schedule, where students are grouped according to the grade level at which they are currently working. Each class's range of content is significantly reduced; for example, some students' understanding of their class's specific content might be at the end-of-fifth-grade level while others in the class may have mastered some sixth-grade standards but not enough to be ready for seventh-grade work. In this scenario, the range of readiness is much narrower than a traditional classroom, and the range of grade levels is minimized, because *all* students in the class are working within the same or very similar set of expectations and have mastered the previous knowledge required for those standards. Imagine what this feels like for educators and students. In our experience teaching within PCBE systems, it feels like a miracle. For this reason, a complete rethinking of the scheduling process may prove to be the driver that ensures success of every other component of implementing PCBE.

Organizing Students Based on Their Learning Needs

Table 1.1 shows how traditional grade levels are organized based on age—the method schools typically use to organize their students into classes. In the PCBE scheduling process, age is a variable that may be taken into account, but it is not the driving force determining a student's location for instruction.

Table 1.1: Grade-Level Breakdown Based on Students' Age

GRADE	TYPICAL AGE RANGE
K	4.9–5.8
1	5.9–6.8
2	6.9–7.8
3	7.9–8.8
4	8.9–9.8
5	9.9–10.8
6	10.9–11.8
7	11.9–12.8
8	12.9–13.8
9	13.9–14.8
10	14.9–15.8
11	15.9–16.8
12	16.9–17.8

Source: Marzano et al., 2017, p. 134.

Comparing data for traditional scheduling (based on age) and data for PCBE scheduling shows an obvious shift in how the students are organized. Table 1.2 shows a hypothetical distribution of five hundred middle school students based on age, and table 1.3 shows a sample distribution of the same students based on academic needs in each of the four main content areas (English language arts, mathematics, science, and social studies). Notice that the PCBE data in table 1.3 acknowledge that students have needs above and below the set middle school grade levels. Additionally, these data allow the school to narrow the range of learning needs in each class even further by dividing many of the grade levels into two sections. The two lowest grade levels are not divided; students who are not yet working within the fifth-grade standards fall into the fourth-grade group.

Table 1.2: Distribution of Five Hundred Middle School Students Based on Age

	SIXTH GRADE	SEVENTH GRADE	EIGHTH GRADE
English Language Arts	183	145	172
Mathematics	183	145	172
Science	183	145	172
Social Studies	183	145	172

Table 1.3: Distribution of Five Hundred Middle School Students Based on Students' Learning Needs

	FOURTH GRADE	FIFTH GRADE	BEGINNING OF SIXTH GRADE	MIDDLE OF SIXTH GRADE	BEGINNING OF SEVENTH GRADE	MIDDLE OF SEVENTH GRADE	BEGINNING OF EIGHTH GRADE	MIDDLE OF EIGHTH GRADE	BEGINNING OF NINTH GRADE	MIDDLE OF NINTH GRADE	BEGINNING OF TENTH GRADE	MIDDLE OF TENTH GRADE
English Language Arts	30	111	83	63	87	50	50	12	9	2	3	0
Mathematics	56	114	105	50	85	24	34	16	11	1	4	0
Science	56	116	82	62	76	32	40	11	16	3	4	2
Social Studies	26	116	58	87	72	71	41	19	9	0	1	0

Note: "Middle of" denotes completion of 25–75 percent of grade-level standards.

In the traditional age-based groups, classroom teachers must identify and try to meet the varying needs of the individual students within each class, all while covering the grade-level content. This is difficult enough even *with* comprehensive assessment data—which most teachers lack in a traditional age-based scheduling system. Without such data, the teachers have to figure out each student's learning gaps on the fly, and then come up with a strategy to address them, if possible, in the context of continuing with grade-level content. A majority of students are not academically ready for grade-level expectations (The Nation's Report Card, 2019), and a school with traditional scheduling often pushes students through grade-level content for which they lack the foundational concepts and gives them a low final grade that hides the specific gaps in their learning.

In contrast, the PCBE approach to scheduling alters instruction because it organizes groups of students around analysis of specific standards-based data. With the PCBE schedule, classes are organized according to students' standards-based needs, which decreases the academic range in each class. The educator knows ahead of time the specific needs of each student in his or her class and has access to these data so he or she can design and organize resources for instructional units, lessons, and projects accordingly. Instruction focuses not on a set of materials the educator needs to cover according to curriculum pacing guides and programs but on what students need to learn and how instruction can best support their learning.

If student data dictate that a few students in the age range traditionally considered as sixth grade (that is, roughly eleven to twelve years old) are ready for seventh-grade mathematics, then they would be placed in the best group to cover that material. If students who are traditionally in the seventh- and eighth-grade age groups also need the seventh-grade mathematics content, then they could be in that same class. So, one seventh-grade mathematics content class could have students ranging in age from slightly under eleven years old to just under fourteen years old.

Supporting Students to Move at an Appropriate Pace

A foundational component of PCBE deals with students working at their appropriate pace throughout their learning. To fully embrace this component of PCBE, schools must make significant changes in the traditional scheduling system to allow students more flexibility within their learning and to better support educators so they can effectively differentiate instruction for their students. In addition to grouping students according to their learning needs, schools must allow for flexible pacing so students can move through the levels of content as they master the standards.

Looking again at the hypothetical seventh-grade mathematics class, would the class be considered a "low" class or a "high" class? Neither. It would be considered a mathematics class that fills the needs of the students who are taking it. This seventh-grade mathematics class would not necessarily follow the traditional pace of covering all of seventh-grade mathematics in a year's time. It would cover the needed standards to the depth of need. For example, students might only need a few lessons on certain content because they have foundational knowledge that supports learning it at a faster rate. Their pace may slow down with other content to allow for additional lessons, practice, and assessments. In other words, the educator paces the class in response to the students.

A common misunderstanding about newly implemented PCBE systems centers on the idea that students are "not allowed" to advance or that they are "held back" to work within "lower" standards. Scheduling students based on their learning needs does not mean that some students are classified as *low performing* and tracked into a less challenging scope and sequence of learning with no chance to advance to another track, or some are classified as *high performing* and placed in a more challenging scope and sequence. Such a duality creates or hinders opportunities for students based on a predetermined interpretation of potential based on how quickly students learn. That approach to organizing students is the opposite of what PCBE is trying to accomplish. PCBE ensures all students have access to the same scope and sequence of standards, with additional time and support or acceleration offered as needed.

Summary

Scheduling differences between the traditional educational system and PCBE are highlighted by the fundamental approach to organizing students. Age is no longer the driving factor. Standards, personalized instruction, student agency, and leadership all play a major role in developing a PCBE schedule. Completely rethinking the scheduling process for PCBE relies on using student data to drive the organization of students within a schedule, which is the topic of the next chapter.

Chapter 2

The Importance of Student Data Within a PCBE System

[My teacher] gives us feedback in the moment, so I know where I am with the target. We can see our progress. I can actually see that I'm learning.

—Ninth-grade student

Student data are at the core of creating a PCBE schedule. As a result, educators and administrators should give special attention to exploring what constitutes PCBE student data and how to collect them. This chapter is devoted to the concept of student data so that schools can establish a solid foundation for PCBE that will allow them to easily move into scheduling students based on their individual standards-based learning needs.

The origins of PCBE started with standards-based education, and standards-based learning and grading remain an important element of PCBE. Standards-based education means that, rather than averaging students' scores on various assignments, teachers score students based on their proficiency in relation to a clear set of standards. Instead of getting a vague omnibus letter grade or percentage score, each student knows where he or she stands relative to each standard within a given subject area and grade level (Marzano et al., 2017). This information guides the learning process for students and their teachers; it also informs the creation of a schoolwide PCBE schedule. It stands to reason, then, that if data about student proficiency with respect to the content standards aren't already available, the district or school will need to collect them before starting the scheduling process.

To help explain how to collect, analyze, and use student data, throughout this chapter and the rest of the book, we will describe an example hypothetical school that we developed to be roughly representative of what educators and administrators might encounter in real life. As there are significant differences in course design and organizational structure between elementary schools and high schools, our main example is a generic middle school. We will discuss specific elementary and high school situations as needed, but in general, this example middle school will convey the key components of creating a PCBE schedule.

According to the Public School Review (n.d.), U.S. schools (elementary, middle, and high schools) had, on average, 503 students in 2018–2019, and in 2020 that increased to 526 students. The National Center for Education Statistics (n.d.a) stated that "the average class size in 2011–2012 was 21.2 pupils for public elementary schools and 26.8 pupils for public secondary schools." Based on that information, our example middle school has a population of five hundred students and a teacher-student ratio of one to twenty-five. With this student population and teacher-student ratio, the school would have approximately twenty teachers covering the four main content areas for instruction. For this example, the twenty teachers have K–8 certifications. Although not every specific situation will align with this example, we believe this hypothetical school is an effective means of illustrating a framework for PCBE scheduling.

When thinking about scheduling within a PCBE system and using student data based on standards, educators and administrators must have the following right from the start.

- A solid understanding of the different sets of student data that schools must use to successfully implement a PCBE schedule
- A starting point when it comes to available student data
- An understanding of how to create and use comprehensive assessments that gather and clarify accurate student data
- Clarity about how and at what rate the shift to a PCBE schedule will occur

The following sections explore all these key aspects of collecting student data for PCBE scheduling.

Defining Student Data Within a PCBE System

Student data in a PCBE system go well beyond the superficial grades of a traditional system. The traditional age-based system generally requires teachers to instruct students according to curriculum pacing guides, which may or may not actually cover what the students are ready to learn. Teachers then give grades to students based on that grade-level curriculum. The grades are most likely an average of unrelated scores, such as tests, homework, behavior, participation, and so on. For example, if a student gets an A in a class, most people would assume that the student is proficient at the standards in that course—but that letter grade could mean many things. Does that A show that the student is actually proficient in the content, or could it mean the student is an efficient test taker or did lots of extra-credit work to bump up the grade? Does it indicate that the student struggles a little with the content but has stellar behavior? Does it indicate that the student knows some higher-grade-level standards for that content area? All these questions go unanswered due to the nature of how the traditional education system organizes and grades learning.

The same thing occurs at the other end of the traditional spectrum. If a student receives a D on a report card, most people would assume that the student has not mastered the knowledge or skills for that class—yet that may not be the case. Does the grade indicate that the student did well on the tests but did not do the homework? Does it indicate that the student has negative behavior, which factors into the overall grade? Does it indicate that the student isn't even proficient in the background standards for a grade-level concept? A student who is not achieving proficiency may have started struggling with the material in previous grade levels and never really learned the content needed for success later. Again, this problem results from a system in which the teacher must teach to the curriculum pacing guide and provide averaged grades related to the age-based curriculum.

To support personalized competency-based learning, educators and students need scores and data that are much more detailed and accurate than traditional omnibus grades. There are two key levels of data for PCBE scheduling.

1. **Grade-level data:** The broader information about which students belong in which specific grade levels based on their proficiency

2. **Specific standards data:** Detailed data about the level of proficiency each individual student has achieved

These two data sets will form the foundation of the scheduling process. The following sections define each one.

Grade-Level Data

Grade-level data broadly show the number of students who are currently working within a particular set of grade-level standards. Table 2.1 shows a data set for our example middle school (five hundred students) across the content areas of English language arts, mathematics, science, and social studies. This data set offers a big-picture view of all the students in relation to all the content areas and grade levels. Later on, this chapter will discuss how schools collect and organize these data (page 37); for now, the focus is to understand how the data show the distribution of students across all grade levels.

Table 2.1: Sample Grade-Level Data for All Middle School Students

	FOURTH GRADE	FIFTH GRADE	BEGINNING OF SIXTH GRADE	MIDDLE OF SIXTH GRADE	BEGINNING OF SEVENTH GRADE	MIDDLE OF SEVENTH GRADE	BEGINNING OF EIGHTH GRADE	MIDDLE OF EIGHTH GRADE	BEGINNING OF NINTH GRADE	MIDDLE OF NINTH GRADE	BEGINNING OF TENTH GRADE	MIDDLE OF TENTH GRADE
English Language Arts	30	111	83	63	87	50	50	12	9	2	3	0
Mathematics	56	114	105	50	85	24	34	16	11	1	4	0
Science	56	116	82	62	76	32	40	11	16	3	4	2
Social Studies	26	116	58	87	72	71	41	19	9	0	1	0

In this example middle school, the actual content the students need to learn spans from fourth grade all the way to tenth grade. A student who would be assigned to the seventh grade by age might still need to learn material related to previous grade-level standards, or might already have mastered upcoming grade-level standards. Standardized test scores often translate this disparity in achievement by labeling the student as "far below grade level," "below grade level," "at grade level," or "above grade level."

Now consider how table 2.1 (page 23) presents the data. Instead of indicating students' age-based grade levels, these grade-level data show what students actually need to learn in comparison to grade-level standards in each content area. These data provide an overview of students' mastery of subject matter at various grade levels as a whole, not their mastery of specific standards within each grade level. This information shows educators and leaders how many students need instruction at each level, which will be important for creating the schoolwide schedule and assigning students to classes.

Note that this table breaks most grade levels into subcategories, as indicated by the column headings. The seventh-grade content is broken up into two categories: (1) beginning of seventh grade and (2) middle of seventh grade. These subdivisions break the whole student population into smaller groups based on rough percentages of how many standards the students have shown proficiency in at certain levels. If a student has mastered all the sixth-grade science standards but no seventh-grade ones, he or she is clearly at the beginning of seventh grade for that content area. Another student may have already mastered about half the seventh-grade science standards, placing him or her solidly within seventh grade. The district team or school team (depending on the extent of PCBE implementation) will need to determine these percentages, ranges, or cut scores for grouping students. This is part of the comprehensive assessment process, which is covered in more detail later in the chapter (page 42).

Looking at seventh grade more closely, we see the grade-level data show that 109 students are working on seventh-grade mathematics standards: 85 students are starting at the beginning of the seventh-grade standards, and 24 students are working somewhere within the seventh-grade standards. To reiterate, the number 109 does not indicate the standards each student needs to address within seventh-grade mathematics. It does not show the students' behavioral needs, and it does not denote the students' ages. It simply indicates that 109 students in this middle school currently need to work on the standards covered in seventh-grade mathematics.

This information is broad but very important because it groups the students and allows for a more strategic approach to identifying students' needs and more accurately placing students within a PCBE schedule. Grade-level data are the starting point for any PCBE schedule because they identify the grade-level groups and show how the whole student population is distributed across all content areas and grade levels. Having identified the grade-level groups, school leaders and educators can then divide those groups into individual classes.

A grade-level data chart like table 2.1 (page 23) would be accompanied by a list of the actual students for each subcategory—a master list of the students' names and needs. Once the grade-level data have shown how school leaders and educators should group students, then a deeper analysis occurs with the specific standards data for each student in the subcategories.

Specific Standards Data

While grade-level data are very broad and are kept on a whole-school level, specific standards data are specific to each individual student. Specific standards data convey all the standards a student has or has not mastered throughout all content areas. As you can imagine, specific standards data cover a lot of information. They require that a school have lists of all the standards and expectations for each content area and grade level. Because standards-based instruction and reporting are key components of PCBE, a school creating a PCBE schedule should have these lists in place. Then, educators and the students themselves can track learning progress against these lists. In a PCBE system, each student receives a score on each standard within a content area and grade level (rather than an average or omnibus grade for a group of standards).

The lists of standards can take all sorts of formats, such as checklists, matrices, or online databases, and may be embedded within learning management systems. This component of scheduling in PCBE is closely tied to how a school or district's reporting system records and represents student learning. There are many systems of tracking student data out there, and advancements in technology are so fast-paced that it makes it impractical to state specific examples. For further information about and examples of reporting in a PCBE system, please see *A Handbook for Personalized Competency-Based Education* (Marzano et al., 2017). No matter which format a school or district uses, the fundamental approach to analyzing the student data is the same.

For the purpose of this book, we use a standards matrix because it clearly indicates the learning expectations and can be represented in digital or print forms. A standards matrix is an organized list of standards for a specific content area within a certain grade level. Both the educator and the student can use the standards matrix to keep track of what standards the student has mastered, is currently working on, or is just starting to learn. Figure 2.1 (page 26) shows an example standards matrix for the Common Core standards for sixth-grade mathematics (National Governors Association Center for Best Practices [NGA] & Council of Chief State School Officers [CCSSO], 2010b).

The standards matrix clarifies the learning expectations for sixth-grade mathematics for both the educator and the students. Every cluster and standard appears individually. Some standards are broken up into smaller chunks of learning, known as *learning indicators*. The indicators are organized as a checklist following the standard with which they are associated. The checklist denotes a student must complete all the learning indicators for that standard to show proficiency.

SIXTH-GRADE MATHEMATICS	ADVANCED	PROFICIENT	WORKING TOWARD	WITH HELP
6.RP.A: Understand ratio concepts and use ratio reasoning to solve problems.				
6.RP.A.1: Understand the concept of a ratio and use ratio language to describe a ratio relationship between two quantities.				
6.RP.A.2: Understand the concept of a unit rate a/b associated with a ratio $a{:}b$ with $b \neq 0$, and use rate language in the context of a ratio relationship.				
6.RP.A.3: Use ratio and rate reasoning to solve real-world and mathematical problems, e.g., by reasoning about tables of equivalent ratios, tape diagrams, double number line diagrams, or equations.				
The student needs to have learned all the following items in order to be proficient at the preceding standard.				
☐ 6.RP.A.3a: Make tables of equivalent ratios relating quantities with whole-number measurements, find missing values in the tables, and plot the pairs of values on the coordinate plane. Use tables to compare ratios.				
☐ 6.RP.A.3b: Solve unit rate problems including those involving unit pricing and constant speed.				
☐ 6.RP.A.3c: Find a percent of a quantity as a rate per 100 (e.g., 30% of a quantity means 30/100 times the quantity); solve problems involving finding the whole, given a part and the percent.				
☐ 6.RP.A.3d: Use ratio reasoning to convert measurement units; manipulate and transform units appropriately when multiplying or dividing quantities.				
6.NS.A: Apply and extend previous understandings of multiplication and division to divide fractions by fractions.				
6.NS.A.1: Interpret and compute quotients of fractions, and solve word problems involving division of fractions by fractions, e.g., by using visual fraction models and equations to represent the problem.				
6.NS.B: Compute fluently with multi-digit numbers and find common factors and multiples.				
6.NS.B.2: Fluently divide multi-digit numbers using the standard algorithm.				
6.NS.B.3: Fluently add, subtract, multiply, and divide multi-digit decimals using the standard algorithm for each operation.				
6.NS.B.4: Find the greatest common factor of two whole numbers less than or equal to 100 and the least common multiple of two whole numbers less than or equal to 12. Use the distributive property to express a sum of two whole numbers 1–100 with a common factor as a multiple of a sum of two whole numbers with no common factor.				

SIXTH-GRADE MATHEMATICS	ADVANCED	PROFICIENT	WORKING TOWARD	WITH HELP
6.NS.C: Apply and extend previous understandings of numbers to the system of rational numbers.				
6.NS.C.5: Understand that positive and negative numbers are used together to describe quantities having opposite directions or values (e.g., temperature above/below zero, elevation above/below sea level, credits/debits, positive/negative electric charge); use positive and negative numbers to represent quantities in real-world contexts, explaining the meaning of 0 in each situation.				
6.NS.C.6: Understand a rational number as a point on the number line. Extend number line diagrams and coordinate axes familiar from previous grades to represent points on the line and in the plane with negative number coordinates.				
The student needs to have learned all the following items in order to be proficient at the preceding standard.				
☐ 6.NS.C.6a: Recognize opposite signs of numbers as indicating locations on opposite sides of 0 on the number line; recognize that the opposite of the opposite of a number is the number itself, e.g., −(−3) = 3, and that 0 is its own opposite.				
☐ 6.NS.C.6b: Understand signs of numbers in ordered pairs as indicating locations in quadrants of the coordinate plane; recognize that when two ordered pairs differ only by signs, the locations of the points are related by reflections across one or both axes.				
☐ 6.NS.C.6c: Find and position integers and other rational numbers on a horizontal or vertical number line diagram; find and position pairs of integers and other rational numbers on a coordinate plane.				
6.NS.C.7: Understand ordering and absolute value of rational numbers.				
The student needs to have learned all the following items in order to be proficient at the preceding standard.				
☐ 6.NS.C.7a: Interpret statements of inequality as statements about the relative position of two numbers on a number line diagram.				
☐ 6.NS.C.7b: Write, interpret, and explain statements of order for rational numbers in real-world contexts.				
☐ 6.NS.C.7c: Understand the absolute value of a rational number as its distance from 0 on the number line; interpret absolute value as magnitude for a positive or negative quantity in a real-world situation.				
☐ 6.NS.C.7d: Distinguish comparisons of absolute value from statements about order.				

continued →

Figure 2.1: Standards matrix for sixth-grade mathematics.

SIXTH-GRADE MATHEMATICS	ADVANCED	PROFICIENT	WORKING TOWARD	WITH HELP
6.EE.A: Apply and extend previous understandings of arithmetic to algebraic expressions.				
6.EE.A.1: Write and evaluate numerical expressions involving whole-number exponents.				
6.EE.A.2: Write, read, and evaluate expressions in which letters stand for numbers.				
The student needs to have learned all the following items in order to be proficient at the preceding standard.				
☐ 6.EE.A.2a: Write expressions that record operations with numbers and with letters standing for numbers.				
☐ 6.EE.A.2b: Identify parts of an expression using mathematical terms (sum, term, product, factor, quotient, coefficient); view one or more parts of an expression as a single entity.				
☐ 6.EE.A.2c: Evaluate expressions at specific values of their variables. Include expressions that arise from formulas used in real-world problems. Perform arithmetic operations, including those involving whole-number exponents, in the conventional order when there are no parentheses to specify a particular order (Order of Operations).				
6.EE.A.3: Apply the properties of operations to generate equivalent expressions.				
6.EE.A.4: Identify when two expressions are equivalent (i.e., when the two expressions name the same number regardless of which value is substituted into them).				
6.EE.B: Reason about and solve one-variable equations and inequalities.				
6.EE.B.5: Understand solving an equation or inequality as a process of answering a question: which values from a specified set, if any, make the equation or inequality true? Use substitution to determine whether a given number in a specified set makes an equation or inequality true.				
6.EE.B.6: Use variables to represent numbers and write expressions when solving a real-world or mathematical problem; understand that a variable can represent an unknown number, or, depending on the purpose at hand, any number in a specified set.				
6.EE.B.7: Solve real-world and mathematical problems by writing and solving equations of the form $x + p = q$ and $px = q$ for cases in which p, q and x are all nonnegative rational numbers.				
6.EE.B.8: Write an inequality of the form $x > c$ or $x < c$ to represent a constraint or condition in a real-world or mathematical problem. Recognize that inequalities of the form $x > c$ or $x < c$ have infinitely many solutions; represent solutions of such inequalities on number line diagrams.				

SIXTH-GRADE MATHEMATICS	ADVANCED	PROFICIENT	WORKING TOWARD	WITH HELP
6.EE.C: Represent and analyze quantitative relationships between dependent and independent variables.				
6.EE.C.9: Use variables to represent two quantities in a real-world problem that change in relationship to one another; write an equation to express one quantity, thought of as the dependent variable, in terms of the other quantity, thought of as the independent variable. Analyze the relationship between the dependent and independent variables using graphs and tables, and relate these to the equation.				
6.G.A: Solve real-world and mathematical problems involving area, surface area, and volume.				
6.G.A.1: Find the area of right triangles, other triangles, special quadrilaterals, and polygons by composing into rectangles or decomposing into triangles and other shapes; apply these techniques in the context of solving real-world and mathematical problems.				
6.G.A.2: Find the volume of a right rectangular prism with fractional edge lengths by packing it with unit cubes of the appropriate unit fraction edge lengths and show that the volume is the same as would be found by multiplying the edge lengths of the prism. Apply the formulas $V = l \, w \, h$ and $V = b \, h$ to find volumes of right rectangular prisms with fractional edge lengths in the context of solving real-world and mathematical problems.				
6.G.A.3: Draw polygons in the coordinate plane given coordinates for the vertices; use coordinates to find the length of a side joining points with the same first coordinate or the same second coordinate. Apply these techniques in the context of solving real-world and mathematical problems.				
6.G.A.4: Represent three-dimensional figures using nets made up of rectangles and triangles, and use the nets to find the surface area of these figures. Apply these techniques in the context of solving real-world and mathematical problems.				

continued →

SIXTH-GRADE MATHEMATICS	ADVANCED	PROFICIENT	WORKING TOWARD	WITH HELP
6.SP.A: Develop understanding of statistical variability.				
6.SP.A.1: Recognize a statistical question as one that anticipates variability in the data related to the question and accounts for it in the answers.				
6.SP.A.2: Understand that a set of data collected to answer a statistical question has a distribution which can be described by its center, spread, and overall shape.				
6.SP.A.3: Recognize that a measure of center for a numerical data set summarizes all of its values with a single number, while a measure of variation describes how its values vary with a single number.				
6.SP.B: Summarize and describe distributions.				
6.SP.B.4: Display numerical data in plots on a number line, including dot plots, histograms, and box plots.				
6.SP.B.5: Summarize numerical data sets in relation to their context, such as by:				
The student needs to have learned all the following items in order to be proficient at the preceding standard.				
☐ 6.SP.B.5a: Reporting the number of observations.				
☐ 6.SP.B.5b: Describing the nature of the attribute under investigation, including how it was measured and its units of measurement.				
☐ 6.SP.B.5c: Giving quantitative measures of center (median and/or mean) and variability (interquartile range and/or mean absolute deviation), as well as describing any overall pattern and any striking deviations from the overall pattern with reference to the context in which the data were gathered.				
☐ 6.SP.B.5d: Relating the choice of measures of center and variability to the shape of the data distribution and the context in which the data were gathered.				

Source for standards: NGA & CCSSO, 2010b.

To indicate and track the students' level of learning for each standard, educators and students can date, shade in, or place a checkmark in one of the matrix's four rightmost columns. This standards matrix uses the following descriptors.

- *Advanced* indicates the student has demonstrated achievement beyond the expectations of the standard.

- *Proficient* indicates the student has demonstrated all expectations of the standard.

- *Working toward* indicates the student has shown partial proficiency of the expectations of the standard.

- *With help* indicates the student has shown some evidence of learning of the expectations of the standard but only with support (Heflebower, Hoegh, & Warrick, 2014).

Figure 2.2 (page 32) highlights a section of the sixth-grade mathematics standards matrix to show how it is organized into clusters, standards, and indicators. The cluster is 6.RP.A: "Understand ratio concepts and use ratio reasoning to solve problems" (NGA & CCSSO, 2010b). There are three standards associated with this cluster of learning: 6.RP.A.1, 6.RP.A.2, and 6.RP.A.3. A student would be scored on each of these standards; if the student is marked proficient in all three standards, then the student is proficient in the cluster. Standard 6.RP.A.3 has four associated learning indicators. The four indicators have checkboxes to their left for acknowledging whether the student has achieved this learning. Once the student achieves the indicators (that is, the boxes are checked), then the student is proficient on standard 6.RP.A.3. If only some indicators are checked, the student is still progressing toward the standard; all the indicators need evidence of learning before the student can be considered proficient on the standard. The note prior to the indicators that states, "The student needs to have learned all the following items in order to be proficient at the preceding standard," is included to emphasize this point and prevent confusion.

A standards matrix represents a student's progress through all the standards for each content area and grade level. The student and educator keep this information up to date to indicate the student's most recent learning or proficiency on standards. Thus, a student's standards matrix always shows where the student has achieved mastery and where the next learning needs to occur. This is represented in figure 2.2 (page 32) by the dates indicating the progression of student learning over time. Related standards are taught together, but students may be proficient on some standards within a cluster before others, as indicated by 6.RP.1 and 6.RP.2 having evidence of proficiency before 6.RP.3. This is also common due to the varied complexity of the standards themselves. For example, 6.RP.1 is merely understanding the language of ratio and proportion whereas 6.RP.3 requires applying one's understanding of ratio and proportion to real-world problems.

A school might use simple three-ring binders or elaborate digital systems to record specific standards data. Students would have a section for each content area they are learning; in the case of standards matrices, each section includes the matrix for the level on which they are currently working. When a

SIXTH-GRADE MATHEMATICS	ADVANCED	PROFICIENT	WORKING TOWARD	WITH HELP
6.RP.A: Understand ratio concepts and use ratio reasoning to solve problems.				
6.RP.A.1: Understand the concept of a ratio and use ratio language to describe a ratio relationship between two quantities.		February 9	February 7	February 5
6.RP.A.2: Understand the concept of a unit rate a/b associated with a ratio $a:b$ with $b \neq 0$, and use rate language in the context of a ratio relationship.		February 12	February 8	February 5
6.RP.A.3: Use ratio and rate reasoning to solve real-world and mathematical problems, e.g., by reasoning about tables of equivalent ratios, tape diagrams, double number line diagrams, or equations.			February 9	February 7

The student needs to have learned all the following items in order to be proficient at the preceding standard.

- ☑ 6.RP.A.3a: Make tables of equivalent ratios relating quantities with whole-number measurements, find missing values in the tables, and plot the pairs of values on the coordinate plane. Use tables to compare ratios.
- ☑ 6.RP.A.3b: Solve unit rate problems including those involving unit pricing and constant speed.
- ☐ 6.RP.A.3c: Find a percent of a quantity as a rate per 100 (e.g., 30% of a quantity means 30/100 times the quantity); solve problems involving finding the whole, given a part and the percent.
- ☐ 6.RP.A.3d: Use ratio reasoning to convert measurement units; manipulate and transform units appropriately when multiplying or dividing quantities.

Source for standards: NGA & CCSSO, 2010b.

Figure 2.2: Section of a standards matrix for sixth-grade mathematics showing a cluster, standards, and indicators.

student demonstrates proficiency in all the standards in a level, then the educator adds the next level's standards matrix, and the student can see all the learning expectations for the new level.

Identifying a Starting Point and Collecting Initial Data

The process for initially establishing accurate student data has many features and variables that are specific to the individual school or district, such as student population; teacher-student ratio; inherent differences between elementary, middle, and high schools; implementation starting points; and available data. While it is impossible to specifically address each of them here, this section is designed to provide general guidance for collecting student data. It is not a step-by-step process for all schools to follow.

As a school or district prepares to shift to a PCBE schedule, it will have three possible starting points in terms of student data.

1. Starting from a standards-based system

2. Starting from a standards-referenced system (where some standards data are collected)

3. Starting from a traditional system (where no standards data are collected)

The following sections detail each of these possibilities.

Starting From a Standards-Based System

If educators have already been teaching and recording student learning based on standards, then the grade-level data and specific standards data already exist and only need to be analyzed to create a PCBE schedule. Leaders and educators may need to organize and refine the data, but they already have the foundational information.

This situation is the best-case scenario, but it is unfortunately uncommon because most school systems do not use standards-based grading and reporting practices. If reporting on proficiency for all standards is indeed your situation, then chapter 3 (page 51) describes your logical next step, but you might find it helpful to continue reading through the rest of this chapter to ensure the collected data are as accurate and organized as possible.

Starting From a Standards-Referenced System

A standards-referenced system scores students based on standards but does not require that students achieve proficiency on all standards before they can move on to the next level of learning (Marzano, 2010). Students remain in age-based grade levels and are scored on the standards for their grade in each content area. Because students can still move through the grade levels without mastering content, this information is not sufficient for grouping students to create a PCBE schedule. A student who scores "with help" on a seventh-grade mathematics standard may have missed concepts in a previous grade that are crucial to success on the seventh-grade standards. Educators must evaluate the student on the lower-grade-level standards to determine where the student was last proficient within that concept and then group the student accordingly.

If a standards-referenced system is your starting point, then you need to establish a more detailed system of determining and recording what students know and do not know. This approach separates academic scores from behavioral scores, meaning that work completion, behavior, and participation do not affect the learning scores for a class or a course. Using standards matrices and ignoring age-based limitations are crucial to determining at what level students were last proficient in their learning. The process of using comprehensive assessments, addressed in the next section, would be a good starting point; individual educators or school teams can break out the information they obtain from these assessments into grade-level data and specific standards-based data.

Starting From a Traditional System

A traditional system of data collection records only very general information about what a student knows and does not know in comparison to standards. Traditional grades average scores across disparate standards, include topics unrelated to knowledge acquisition (such as behavior), and do not indicate what a student still needs to learn in order to reach proficiency on specific standards. Generally, the most useful data from a traditional system come in the form of standardized testing data, district testing data, and classroom scores, which may or may not be aligned with standards.

If this is your starting point, you will need to begin by collecting more accurate data and aligning data systems with specific standards. Starting from a traditional system means that you will need to establish the foundation of a PCBE system before jumping into creating a PCBE schedule. Utilizing the framework for PCBE in *A Handbook for Personalized Competency-Based Education* (Marzano et al., 2017) will be helpful moving forward.

Establishing Student Data Based on Comprehensive Assessments

No matter your starting point, the use of comprehensive assessments is very beneficial. Assessments are a powerful tool in establishing or verifying initial standards-based student data. Every school needs to know what all the students know (and what they don't know) within all subject areas.

Though determining student knowledge sounds like a daunting process, it can be done. Schools need only perform such large-scale data gathering for all their students at the beginning of the transition to a PCBE system. Once they collect the initial student data, they continually accumulate data each school year, building a longitudinal picture of student progress. Students' data are stored and shared with all their future educators. In this way, the student data become a learning archive containing all the standards students have learned.

After a school has established and deployed its systemwide process to identify where students are within the standards, comprehensive data gathering only needs to occur when new students transfer in from traditional systems. At the initial transition to PCBE, the school can consider all students "transfer students" from the traditional system, so it needs to identify more accurate student data for all of them. Then in the future, educators can perform additional data-gathering assessments annually to augment the initial data, but they can make these assessments more targeted.

The process described here—using comprehensive assessments to establish grade-level data and specific standards data—is a starting point for schools wishing to collect comprehensive data without a lengthy data-gathering period. Though not a perfect system, it is a more accurate process for determining what students know and do not know based on the standards than a traditional data-gathering system is. Schools can and should modify this process to fit their specific needs. They should always customize processes to best suit specific situations. Most importantly, stakeholders should understand the reason for the process, and they should use the data effectively.

The following sections explore how to transition to comprehensive assessments, how to address grade-level data, and how to address specific standards data as part of this process.

How to Transition to Comprehensive Assessments

Comprehensive assessments must exist for all grade levels and for all content areas. Generally speaking, a comprehensive assessment is a collection of test questions aligned to the entire set of grade-level standards expectations. This may be given as a single cumulative test or in a series of smaller tests given over time—for example, quarterly. When administered to a student, a comprehensive assessment helps identify initial starting points within the range of standards that are covered.

Due to comprehensive assessments' nature and their use across the entire system, traditional selected-response and constructed-response tests (presented on paper or digitally) are especially helpful as comprehensive assessments because of their continuity of approach, ease of scoring, and familiarity to students. (The following section, page 37, describes how to use traditional comprehensive tests in determining initial student data.) However, it is good to keep in mind that assessments within a PCBE system have a greater emphasis on student engagement and choice. Generally, we recommend that schools expand assessment opportunities beyond traditional tests and incorporate more nontraditional assessments such as probing discussions, demonstrations, observations, and student-generated assessments (Marzano et al., 2017).

Regardless of the specific structure or style of test, the work of building comprehensive assessments can and should be done collectively and shared throughout all grade levels within a school and even across an entire district. Though all staff who instruct students in any capacity need to be able to develop classroom assessments aligned to individual standards, we recommend having a select team of interested and skilled staff work collaboratively on the comprehensive assessments. This might take the form of grade-level teams working across all content areas for elementary generalists, or content-area teams focusing on multiple grade levels within, say, mathematics, in middle or high schools. Once this team has drafted the assessments, there should be a review period in which all staff have the opportunity to give feedback. The design team then revises the comprehensive assessments before final adoption and deployment takes place. An ongoing review cycle (for example, annually or every two years) should be developed to ensure accuracy and alignment of the comprehensive assessments over time. Richard DuFour, Rebecca DuFour, and Robert Eaker (2007) outlined their case for common assessments by emphasizing that working in teams is efficient, it is more equitable for students, and it builds staff capacity. This work undoubtedly helps build inter-rater reliability, but it also helps the team develop systemic skills and processes that aid in improving student learning.

To return to our example middle school transitioning to a PCBE system, such a school needs to create comprehensive standards-based assessments for all sixth-, seventh-, and eighth-grade content areas. Also, because the traditional system allows for potentially large educational gaps to form, the school needs to create comprehensive assessments below the typical middle school grades—assessments that might cover third-, fourth-, and fifth-grade standards, depending on the extent of the gaps. Further, some students' knowledge may go beyond the middle school grade levels; therefore, the school might also need to develop assessments for ninth and tenth grades and possibly beyond. In the case of an all-PCBE district, the school could simply borrow lower or higher grade-level assessments used in other schools.

This transition requires a lot of up-front work, but that work is necessary to have a more efficient process in the long run. The development of comprehensive assessments, as mentioned before, is best done by teams of interested and skilled staff. These teams use a blended approach of identifying assessment resources, vetting the resources for alignment, and creating new assessment items. For example, teams might analyze released assessment items from their state, provincial, or national department of education, and district or school resources such as end-of-level exams, adopted testing platforms, or curriculum resources. Where they find gaps, the team creates new assessment items based on the expectation of each standard. Keeping in mind that many standards are complex and require multiple assessment items, developing additional assessment items might also be the case when there are not enough to adequately determine student proficiency on a standard.

The comprehensive assessment process piggybacks on other components of the PCBE system, such as establishing clearly defined learning standards and creating, aligning, and implementing classroom assessments (Marzano et al., 2017). Effective comprehensive assessments use the standards themselves in their design, and schools need to unpack the standards with the proper level of rigor identified for a proficient score. For more details on creating comprehensive assessments, see *The New Art and Science of Classroom Assessment* by Robert J. Marzano, Jennifer S. Norford, and Mike Ruyle (2019). The end goal is to have one large assessment or a collection of smaller assessments for each content area at each grade level that districts and schools can give to determine a baseline of students' current learning in relation to the standards.

To ease their workload, school or district teams could spread out the development of all the comprehensive assessments over time. Additionally, PCBE scheduling might begin with only one or two content areas, which would allow school or district teams to create additional content-area assessments at a later time. Some content areas are more conducive to larger comprehensive assessments than others due to the nature of their standards. For example, mathematics is often an easier place to start with comprehensive assessments than English language arts (ELA), as ELA requires writing samples and a variety of texts. ELA tests might also be more labor intensive to administer and score.

Please note that research indicates using only one assessment to determine proficiency is not particularly reliable or accurate, and a collection of evidence is always recommended over one isolated assessment score (Marzano et al., 2019). However, at the beginning of the transition to PCBE, schools may have little accurate standards-based data. The use of comprehensive assessments to place students is a starting point. The comprehensive assessments help get students into classes that focus on their needs, and then educators collect formative data—perhaps from exit tickets, probing discussions, quick checks for understanding, and so on—as well as summative data—from cumulative traditional tests or in-depth projects—to support and refine the students' placement. If evidence shows that a comprehensive assessment has placed a student in the wrong class, educators and school leaders can rectify the situation, ideally within the first few weeks of the course.

With comprehensive assessments created for all content areas and grade levels, schools now have a foundation to initially collect student data. The results from a comprehensive assessment directly translate into the two sets of data discussed previously: (1) grade-level data and (2) specific standards data.

How to Address Grade-Level Data

Grade-level data from comprehensive assessments deal with students' overall results on the assessments. Once students have taken the comprehensive assessments, schools should use the grade-level data to divide the students into three general categories.

1. Proficient on less than 25 percent of the standards

2. Proficient on between 25 percent and 75 percent of the standards

3. Proficient on more than 75 percent of the standards

Each range indicates students have scored proficient on a certain percentage of the standards that the comprehensive assessment covers for a certain grade level in a particular content area. These ranges are the indicators at which students are determined to be proficient or not proficient in a level—for the comprehensive assessment process. Schools and districts can adopt these ranges described here or establish their own, with the understanding that it is meant to be a flexible system to best support student learning. The ranges help schools place students within grade levels and determine if students need to take comprehensive assessments from higher or lower grade levels to find out the full scope of what they do or do not know within a content area.

The following sections concern how educators should address students whose comprehensive assessment results fall into these three categories.

Proficient on Less Than 25 Percent of the Standards

A student who scores proficient on less than 25 percent of the standards on a given grade level's comprehensive assessment for a specific content area should most likely be placed in that grade level for that content area. However, the student should also take the comprehensive assessment for the preceding grade level to ensure there are no learning gaps.

For example, imagine a student demonstrates proficiency on 15 percent of the standards for eighth-grade science. This student would most likely attend a class that addresses eighth-grade science standards. However, a score below 25 percent on the eighth-grade comprehensive assessment also indicates that the student should take the seventh-grade science comprehensive assessment to get additional information about the last place of proficiency. Educators know the student is not proficient on a majority of the eighth-grade standards, but there are additional unknown data that the educators need to gather. They must answer the question, Is the student missing knowledge needed to be successful on the eighth-grade science standards? Taking the seventh-grade comprehensive assessment for science adds more evidence to the grade-level data.

Typically, students will show a variability of proficiency across different content areas. Students who show 10 percent standards proficiency on their comprehensive mathematics assessment may very well show 65 percent standards proficiency on their comprehensive ELA assessment at the same grade level, or vice versa. Therefore, additional lower- or higher-level assessment administration occurs according to need because the data on the student's needs drive course assignment. The student's age is irrelevant—perhaps the aforementioned student would be in ninth grade in the traditional age-based system, but the comprehensive assessment shows a lack of proficiency on the majority of the eighth-grade standards in science. This does not mean the student repeats eighth grade—or even eighth-grade science—from beginning to end, unless the data show that the student has not completed any of the eighth-grade standards. For students who have shown some proficiency, their teachers are responsible for personalizing instruction and presenting the standards they still need to learn. Once a student has shown proficiency on all the eighth-grade standards in a content area, that student advances directly on to ninth-grade standards; the learning is not bound by the 180-day school year or any curriculum pacing guide.

Proficient on Between 25 Percent and 75 Percent of the Standards

A comprehensive assessment score between 25 percent and 75 percent proficiency indicates significant gaps within the tested grade level and content area for that student. Educators need to identify and fill in the learning gaps before addressing content at the next level up. They should most likely place the student in a group that addresses the tested grade level's standards for this content area and not advance to the next level at this time. As noted in the previous section, the student focuses on just the missing standards and then moves to the next level. The shift from, for example, eighth-grade standards to ninth-grade standards will be faster in this situation because fewer eighth-grade standards remain to complete the level of learning. It is rare that a student knows nothing of the content-area requirements, so any current skills or understanding increases the learning pace through the standards.

Students who score at the edges of this range (that is, close to 25 percent or close to 75 percent) require flexibility. Because they are right on the verge, additional information, such as observation, discussion, or another assessment point, is helpful to ensure the best academic fit.

Proficient on More Than 75 Percent of the Standards

A comprehensive assessment score above 75 percent proficiency indicates that a student is ready or nearly ready for the next level of standards in that content area. Educators or school teams could place the student in a group that covers the next level of standards with an understanding that instruction may need to address a few small gaps in the previous standards. The student who scores above 75 percent should also take the comprehensive assessment for the next level in that content area to find out if the student is proficient at any of those standards. The goal of the comprehensive assessment process is to find out what students know and don't know in comparison to the standards, and taking the next-level comprehensive assessment will provide more detailed data about the student's learning and allow the teacher to focus instruction more efficiently. Wherever teachers can increase pacing through targeting instruction, student gaps will fill faster, and achievement will rise.

Table 2.2 (page 40) shows grade-level data from our example middle school, which used the comprehensive assessment categories and criteria to create the groups within each column. The number in each column indicates how many students are assigned to that level of standards. As an example, consider the following assessment process for students who would be in sixth grade by age. Students who received a comprehensive score between 25 percent and 75 percent on the sixth-grade mathematics assessment are placed in the "Middle of Sixth Grade" group for that content area. They are working within the sixth-grade standards and need to complete those areas before moving to seventh-grade mathematics. Students who scored below 25 percent on the sixth-grade mathematics comprehensive assessment then took the fifth-grade comprehensive assessment. If the students' scores on the fifth-grade assessment exceeded 75 percent, then they best fit in the "Beginning of Sixth Grade" group for mathematics. This means they have acquired enough fifth-grade content to start tackling the sixth-grade standards. Students who scored higher than 75 percent on the sixth-grade mathematics comprehensive assessment had an opportunity to take the seventh-grade comprehensive assessment. If they then scored between 25 percent and 75 percent on the seventh-grade assessment, then they are placed in the "Middle of Seventh Grade" group for mathematics. Using the comprehensive assessment scores for all the students provides more accurate grade-level data for the entire school.

Table 2.2: Grade-Level Data for All Middle School Students in Mathematics

FOURTH GRADE	FIFTH GRADE	BEGINNING OF SIXTH GRADE	MIDDLE OF SIXTH GRADE	BEGINNING OF SEVENTH GRADE	MIDDLE OF SEVENTH GRADE	BEGINNING OF EIGHTH GRADE	MIDDLE OF EIGHTH GRADE	BEGINNING OF NINTH GRADE	MIDDLE OF NINTH GRADE	BEGINNING OF TENTH GRADE	MIDDLE OF TENTH GRADE
56	114	105	50	85	24	34	16	11	1	4	0

Keep in mind that these initial data represent a starting point for the PCBE system. A school has to start somewhere, and this process gives a much more accurate picture than the traditional system's assumption that age corresponds to grade-level proficiency of the standards. Once a school is consistently recording student learning based on standards, its grade-level data will be much more accurate and easier to compile.

How to Address Specific Standards Data

Educators or school teams can also use comprehensive assessment results to determine specific standards data for each student. Recording specific standards data deals with the specific assessment questions that align with each standard. This is a fairly straightforward process as long as schools or districts design the comprehensive assessments to be fair (lacking biases), valid (measuring what they say they measure), and reliable (consistent; Marzano, 2010).

When designing the actual questions on a comprehensive assessment, schools or districts need to ensure all questions align with specific standards. No hard-and-fast rule exists for how many questions should represent one particular standard; the standard itself will drive the number of questions needed. One question is rarely enough evidence, but fifteen questions, say, may be excessive. You have to take into consideration the complexity of the standard for both depth and breadth of coverage. For example, standards may cover multiple indicators, as in the case of the ratios and proportions mathematics standard in figure 2.2 (page 32). These obviously will require additional questions to adequately address all the knowledge and content, but even less complex standards often need several questions to cover the depth or breadth of the expectations. Consider a second-grade standard requiring students to tell and write time to the nearest five minutes from analog and digital clocks. This is a fairly focused standard, but still involves several components. To generate sufficient evidence about what students know and can do on this standard, a comprehensive assessment would require questions that include both analog and digital clocks as well as opportunities to both tell and write time.

Since the comprehensive assessment consists of groups of questions that collectively cover all the standards for a particular content area and grade level, the assessment needs to be balanced so it results in enough specific evidence for each standard. This is why comprehensive assessments are large and might be broken up into segments and administered in multiple sessions—though educators should certainly aim to keep the tests reasonable in length. Comprehensive assessments should also be organized for ease of scoring and analysis, so all questions related to a particular standard should be grouped together. Related standards within strands of learning should also be grouped together; for example, all the ratios and proportions standards would be in the same section of the assessment. This makes it easier to score and to break the test up into chunks if need be.

Just as they set ranges for the grade-level data, schools need to set ranges for the specific standards data. These are harder to establish because there are fewer data points to take into account. For example, six questions may represent the proficiency expectations for one standard on a certain grade-level comprehensive assessment. Keeping to similar ranges as used for grade-level data (0–24 percent, 25–75 percent, and 76–100 percent), if a student got four of the six questions correct, he or she would have 67 percent of the questions on that standard correct, which would not qualify as mastery in most cases. So this would indicate that a student is "working toward" those learning expectations. But it also signals that the school needs to gather additional evidence, as the student has mastered many expectations of the standard. This is why we recommend a range rather than a hard-and-fast cut score. If a student is close to edge of a range, additional data will help ensure the student is placed correctly.

Different types of questions may provide more or less evidence than others and be a clearer indicator of proficiency. For example, a constructed response question gives students much more opportunity to share their knowledge and skills than a multiple-choice question, so the body of evidence gathered may vary from comprehensive test to comprehensive test, and the scoring for specific standards data might differ based on the standards' types and numbers of questions. Always keep this question in mind when developing and scoring comprehensive assessments: Will this assessment offer enough evidence that a student knows enough to be successful in the next level of this learning expectation?

During the initial placement process, educators give students the comprehensive tests, often in age-based classrooms. In order to clarify the specific standards data, these educators can transfer the results from a comprehensive assessment directly to a standards matrix. All questions that students answer correctly on the assessment indicate some evidence of learning ranging from "with help" to "proficient." If there is enough evidence to show proficiency for a particular standard, then the educator can place a checkmark or date in the corresponding "proficient" box on the standards matrix. At this point, there is no need to focus on the advanced level of proficiency because the initial stage of data collection emphasizes what students know up to proficiency, which is enough to initially group the students.

Remember that comprehensive assessments are primarily used to assist in the better placement of students, not necessarily to score and report officially on proficiency. Once a student is placed, educators can and should use additional time to gather more accurate data on students during the buffer period of the first few instructional weeks. So, while sites should try to develop the most aligned comprehensive tests for each content area and grade level, they should keep in mind that this is a mere dipstick into what a student knows and is able to do across the breadth of a grade-level content area. Educators will collect more classroom evidence to back up these initial comprehensive test data.

Figure 2.3 shows how educators can fill in a standards matrix using these data. In this example, there is evidence from the sixth-grade mathematics comprehensive assessment to indicate that the student is proficient on these standards—the student scored above 80 percent for both standards 6.RP.A.1 and 6.RP.A.2. The dates indicate when the comprehensive test was administered. The evidence from the comprehensive assessment also indicates that the student received a score of 50 percent on the questions aligned to standard 6.RP.A.3 and therefore is "working toward" proficiency of that standard. The correct answers on 6.RP.A.3 show that the student does know two of the four indicators covered by that standard, which is why those two indicators are checked.

Continuing this process for all matrices that correspond to the comprehensive assessments will create the initial specific standards data for each student in each content area and grade level.

Collecting Student Data for PCBE Scheduling

In this section, we present three approaches to collecting student data for the transition to a PCBE schedule, but this process is not limited to just these three. Schools and districts can combine or otherwise customize the approaches to meet their needs related to developing student data. Once the school or district has transitioned to a PCBE system, this process of collecting data would not need to be done again systemwide, since yearly standards-based progress data for students is available to the upcoming grade-level educator each successive year. These three approaches focus on the timeline for administering the comprehensive assessments and the time needed to analyze the results to determine the grade-level data and specific standards data.

1. Collect data at the end of a school year for the next school year.

2. Collect data at the start of a school year for that current school year.

3. Collect data throughout a school year for the next school year.

Each approach has advantages and disadvantages. In the following sections, we discuss each of these approaches to gathering academic data, as well as the role of behavioral data.

SIXTH-GRADE MATHEMATICS	ADVANCED	PROFICIENT	WORKING TOWARD	WITH HELP
6.RP.A: Understand ratio concepts and use ratio reasoning to solve problems.				
6.RP.A.1: Understand the concept of a ratio and use ratio language to describe a ratio relationship between two quantities.		September 9		
6.RP.A.2: Understand the concept of a unit rate a/b associated with a ratio $a:b$ with $b \neq 0$, and use rate language in the context of a ratio relationship.		September 9		
6.RP.A.3: Use ratio and rate reasoning to solve real-world and mathematical problems, e.g., by reasoning about tables of equivalent ratios, tape diagrams, double number line diagrams, or equations.			September 9	

The student needs to have learned all the following items in order to be proficient at the preceding standard.

☑ 6.RP.A.3a: Make tables of equivalent ratios relating quantities with whole-number measurements, find missing values in the tables, and plot the pairs of values on the coordinate plane. Use tables to compare ratios.

☑ 6.RP.A.3b: Solve unit rate problems including those involving unit pricing and constant speed.

☐ 6.RP.A.3c: Find a percent of a quantity as a rate per 100 (e.g., 30% of a quantity means 30/100 times the quantity); solve problems involving finding the whole, given a part and the percent.

☐ 6.RP.A.3d: Use ratio reasoning to convert measurement units; manipulate and transform units appropriately when multiplying or dividing quantities.

Source for standard: NGA & CCSSO, 2010b.

Figure 2.3: Section of a standards matrix for sixth-grade mathematics showing specific standards data from a comprehensive assessment.

Collecting Data at the End of the Year

The process of collecting data at the end of a school year for the upcoming school year uses comprehensive assessments as the starting point. At the end of the academic year, during the last month of school, all students take comprehensive assessments on all the standards within their grade level for the content areas that will be the focus of the PCBE schedule. Some schools may take an incremental approach to the transition to PCBE, scheduling PCBE in just one or two content areas for the upcoming school year, so they give only those comprehensive assessments. The comprehensive assessment results then determine the grade-level data and specific standards data.

An advantage to this approach is that it allows the current teacher who has instructed the students throughout the course of the year to administer the comprehensive tests. This educator has a great deal of knowledge about what students know and are able to do regardless of whether or not the educator has been specifically recording and reporting information about each student's performance on all standards. Leaving data collection to the end of the year provides additional opportunities for educators to add feedback and evidence about what they know about students in relation to the standards covered in the comprehensive assessment. Another benefit of this approach is that the school has the end of the year and the summer to analyze the data, organize students based on their needs, and schedule classes appropriately. So, this approach starts during the last month of the school year and continues throughout the summer, making it about a three-month initial process.

A disadvantage to this approach is that, as with any comprehensive assessment process, schools need to conduct a lot of testing. This process only needs to happen once, at the beginning of the transition to PCBE, for the entire student population and need not be repeated in upcoming years, but it is time consuming at first. Lastly, giving an assessment at year's end does not account for loss of knowledge and skills over the summer and therefore may not be as accurate a measure at the start of the following school year.

Collecting Data at the Start of the Year

This approach uses the beginning of the school year for data collection, during the first two to three weeks of school, with the comprehensive assessments immediately administered and analyzed for scheduling. Students take the comprehensive assessments that address the content they learned in the previous school year. The results of this establish what the students know and do not know in preparation for the current year's learning.

For example, at the beginning of a school year, a ninth-grade-age student takes the comprehensive assessment on eighth-grade content to identify readiness for the ninth-grade standards. This is more useful than taking a ninth-grade assessment because the student has not received instruction on the ninth-grade standards; the results from that assessment would likely indicate that the student does not know any ninth-grade standards, and they would not indicate what, if anything, the student knows about the eighth-grade standards. At the initial phase of PCBE, the school needs to determine what students have already mastered, so providing comprehensive assessments based on the standards that students should already know is much more informative. These tests are diagnostic in nature, meant to identify where there are gaps as well as where strengths lie.

An advantage to this approach is its shorter timeline for implementing a PCBE schedule. Planning, conversations, training, and the creation of the comprehensive assessments can occur at the end of the previous year and throughout the summer. This allows the school staff to work on the transition without having school actively in session. Also, this approach allows educators to pinpoint in real time where students are in their learning at the start of the school year. Often the beginning of the year, when students take all the assessments, is devoted to building relationships rather than to teaching content, so testing can be interspersed throughout the first week or two with less impact on instruction.

A disadvantage to this approach is the use of a single comprehensive assessment, as explained previously. This approach also necessitates a quick turnaround for organizing students based on their comprehensive assessment scores, after the substantial amount of testing that needs to occur at the beginning of the school year. Another disadvantage of collecting data at the beginning of the year is it may seem as if students have less proficiency than is truly the case; sometimes, students just need a refresher on certain content due to summer learning loss.

Collecting Data Throughout the Year

Collecting data throughout the academic year is different from the other two approaches because it does not rely on assessments given at a single point in time. Rather, educators collect evidence through standards-based instruction and assessment over the course of an entire school year. If they need additional data points to provide a clear picture of where students are in the learning, they can still give comprehensive assessments to add to the body of evidence. To transition to PCBE, students learn the grade-level standards for their age-based group throughout the final year of the traditional system, resulting in significant evidence from which to form student groups for the first year of PCBE. This approach requires that the school and staff have already adopted some level of the standards-referenced approach, with instruction, assessment, and recording aligned to standards. Whereas the previous approaches allowed for educators to move toward competency-based education throughout the year after assessments are given, this approach places the comprehensive assessment process as a final check for understanding following an entire year of data gathering in relation to each standard within age-based classrooms.

An advantage to this approach is that it creates the most reliable and comprehensive student data for developing a PCBE schedule. The data collected throughout the year are much more accurate than those gleaned from a single comprehensive assessment. It is more reliable to gather multiple sets of evidence, which give more information and provide trajectories of student learning, than to rely on one assessment where the risk of anomalous or unclear data is higher. Educators have ample time to instruct, gather evidence, and work collaboratively to develop accurate data. It also allows schools to plan and train staff and students to be better prepared for a PCBE system.

A disadvantage to this approach is the amount of preparation needed. All educators must successfully teach to all the standards and record students' proficiency on all standards covered throughout the school year. The preparation for this year of collecting data may actually start the year before, so the timeline on this approach is much longer. This approach interweaves with a school's systems for grading and reporting student learning. Again, the data-collection year essentially involves standards-referenced instruction, grading, and reporting. The school may formalize these changes and move to a standards-referenced report card during this initial year or may choose a hybrid model. For example, teachers might record standards-based data for internal use and report traditional grades on the formal report card, or they might record and report both traditional grades and proficiency scores simultaneously as part of the transition year, keeping in mind that this may be more transparent for stakeholders but would be more work for educators. Thus, this approach lends itself to a two-year transition to PCBE: shifting to standards-referenced systems in the first year and creating PCBE schedules and pacing in the second year.

It's easy to see that any approach to transitioning to a PCBE schedule is many-tiered and complex. It also involves some degree of ambiguity, which, though part of all major change, can be a powerful distractor and halt progress, causing schools or districts to wait for the "right" answer. Schools or districts must realize that they have to establish a starting point for student data. Though no one approach is going to be perfect, this should not prevent schools from moving forward in the PCBE scheduling process. Finding the best fit for each school's particular strengths, culture, and needs is part of the process. The thought, "We will not move forward unless we have a perfectly designed process," is unrealistic and also drains important focus and energy from the purpose for implementation the staff identified in the first place—positively affecting students. As our former superintendent, John Davis, used to say, "It's about the kids." Schools have used the traditional system for over a hundred years, and it is far from perfect. Do not let perfect be the enemy of good. Rather, do your best to collect the best data available at the most appropriate rate.

Table 2.3 shows the grade-level data for our example middle school's five hundred sixth-, seventh-, and eighth-grade students in all content areas. This chart is a culmination of all the data that the school needs to collect to inform the creation of a PCBE schedule. The example school used the third approach (collecting data throughout the year) as it establishes the most reliable student data to create a PCBE schedule. This data collection is continual throughout students' learning, and the data are recorded and viewed by future teachers, by parents or caregivers, and by the students themselves in an ongoing manner. As described previously, students take a comprehensive assessment for each content area, with the levels of the initial tests being determined by their current age-based grade level. The results of those initial assessments determine placement or additional testing. Students who score

Table 2.3: Grade-Level Data Based on Comprehensive Assessment Results for All Middle School Students in ELA, Mathematics, Science, and Social Studies

	FOURTH GRADE (0–25% on fifth-grade standards)	FIFTH GRADE (25–75% on the fifth-grade standards)	SIXTH GRADE Beginning (0–25% on the sixth-grade standards)	SIXTH GRADE Middle (25–75% on the sixth-grade standards)	SEVENTH GRADE Beginning (0–25% on the seventh-grade standards)	SEVENTH GRADE Middle (25–75% on the seventh-grade standards)	EIGHTH GRADE Beginning (0–25% on the eighth-grade standards)	EIGHTH GRADE Middle (25–75% on the eighth-grade standards)	NINTH GRADE Beginning (0–25% on the ninth-grade standards)	NINTH GRADE Middle (25–75% on the ninth-grade standards)	TENTH GRADE Beginning (0–25% on the tenth-grade standards)	TENTH GRADE Middle (25–75% on the tenth-grade standards)
SIXTH-GRADE-AGED STUDENTS (183)												
ELA	28	86	41	15	8	3	2	0	0	0	0	0
Mathematics	54	69	44	7	5	3	1	0	0	0	0	0
Science	55	66	31	14	10	4	3	0	0	0	0	0
Social Studies	26	92	26	23	6	5	5	0	0	0	0	0
SEVENTH-GRADE-AGED STUDENTS (145)												
ELA	2	19	27	42	31	12	5	3	4	0	0	0
Mathematics	2	42	33	22	28	7	5	3	3	0	0	0
Science	1	45	38	11	30	6	6	4	4	0	0	0
Social Studies	0	22	14	57	16	25	5	2	4	0	0	0
EIGHTH-GRADE-AGED STUDENTS (172)												
ELA	0	6	15	6	48	35	43	9	5	2	3	0
Mathematics	0	3	28	21	52	14	28	13	8	1	4	0
Science	0	5	13	37	36	22	31	7	12	3	4	2
Social Studies	0	2	18	7	50	41	31	17	5	0	1	0

in the central range (proficient on 25–75 percent of standards) of a given grade level can be placed in that grade level for that content area without additional testing. Students who demonstrate a high level of proficiency in a content area would take the test for the next level up, while students whose results indicate they may not be ready for the assessed level take the test for the preceding level. To narrow the range of learning needs in classes, most grade levels are divided into beginning (students who are just starting to work on those standards) and middle (students who are well on their way and have mastered some standards).

Collecting Student Behavioral Data

In addition to all the academic data that they need to collect for each student, schools must take into account students' behavioral data. *Behavioral data* is a general term for a student's social, emotional, and environmental needs, and taking behavioral data into account means that those needs must be part of the scheduling equation. Behavioral data might include a variety of input from formal discipline reports, student history, observational data, surveys, and everything in between. Behavioral IEPs with accommodations for students receiving special education services are also part of behavioral data collection when thinking of scheduling. With all the potential sources and types of behavioral data available, this area might vary widely from school to school or even within a school.

It is important to note that schools should always begin the scheduling process with academic data for all students, with behavioral data as a secondary consideration. While PCBE systems consider the whole student and generally avoid making decisions based on a singular point of reference, student academic data are the main focus for PCBE scheduling. Accurate, standards-based data are the best starting point for organizing the students; from there, schools can filter the initial grouping of students through behavioral data. This filtering process may include looking at disciplinary referrals (ideally from multiple years) to determine if certain students learn better together and with which teachers. Educators might also review behavioral data to see how student motivation is impacted by challenge levels. Some students respond more positively to higher levels of challenge and seek to push themselves, while others might struggle more and feel overwhelmed. If a student possesses a fixed mindset or low grit in a content area—as identified through teacher observation, student self-reporting, or a specific assessment (see Mindset Works, 2017, and Duckworth, 2020, respectively)—placement in a more challenging environment could have a strong negative impact on the student's learning. So, when additional behavioral data such as these are available, through surveys or other means, it can support decision making. This should not be an unduly lengthy process, though, because schools will organize most students primarily based on their academic data; few students have behavioral needs so severe that they take priority over academic needs.

If, for example, student academic data show that two students should be placed in the same classroom, but discipline referral data make it apparent that behavioral issues (such as fighting or bullying) will affect their learning and the class as a whole, the behavioral data may take priority over the academic data. In such a case, the behavioral component will determine a student's placement, while still maintaining the closest academic fit possible. Additionally, if academic data suggest a placement that creates a large disparity in age within a classroom—for example, a ten-year-old whose comprehensive assessment results place her in eighth-grade ELA—decisions around social, emotional, and developmental appropriateness may dictate placement. These situations warrant conversations with the student and the student's caregivers and educators to discuss the student's overall well-being and determine if the age range is appropriate and supportive of student learning. Schools can take into account academic, behavioral, social-emotional, and physical needs when making placement decisions.

The general rule of "academic data first, behavioral data second" still applies when considering students with IEPs. According to the U.S. Department of Education (2019), IEPs should be designed around students' strengths and other factors such as state or district test scores, caregiver input, and recent classroom evaluations in order to help the students "advance toward the annual goals" and "be involved in and progress in the general curriculum." Because the general curriculum is framed around state, provincial, or national standards, the special education team, with input from students and caregivers, develop measurable goals that align with the standards to enhance student learning, and they also identify the least restrictive environment in which this learning can take place. Obviously, schools need to follow all rules and regulations in accordance with both state or provincial and federal laws.

Summary

Student data encompass much more than just an averaged grade. They give information about what students have learned in relation to all content-area standards across all completed grade levels, as well as the level in which they are currently working. For the purpose of scheduling, decision makers need to understand two sets of student data: (1) grade-level data and (2) specific standards data. Grade-level data identify what grade level students are working in and whether they are just starting that level or have mastered some of the standards already. These data help group students based on their broader needs within a content area. Specific standards data reflect which individual standards within a content-area level a student has mastered or to what degree, if mastery has not yet been achieved. Behavioral data can also be used as an additional filter in special cases where academic need is moderated or superseded by behavioral factors.

Schools should develop and use comprehensive assessments aligned to content-area and grade-level expectations to initially group students according to academic needs. The rate at which a school transitions to a PCBE schedule defines when and how to give comprehensive assessments to students—at the beginning or end of a school year, or as an additional final check to add to data collected throughout the year. These data, aligned to standards, allow for more accurate placement of students, which in turn creates the best environment for student learning and reduces the range of content teachers need to address. Data gathering is a foundational component of successful PCBE scheduling and helps drive the design process outlined in the next chapter.

Chapter 3

An Overview of PCBE Scheduling

*Since everyone has a different pace, [PCBE] allows us to not go too fast or too slow.
It helps everyone in a different way because people can be ahead and help or take
more time. We try to support everyone so we can all get to a good place and succeed in
our learning.*

—Ninth-grade student

In a PCBE system, academic and behavioral data for each student are the foundation for creating the schoolwide schedule and determining where students should be located during certain class periods. If these data are absent, then schools have no foundation on which to create a PCBE schedule, and they should collect the most accurate student data possible (as described in chapter 2, page 21) before pursuing PCBE scheduling.

This chapter provides an overview of PCBE scheduling options and considerations. The following sections address designing, transitioning to, and fine-tuning a PCBE schedule, as well as regrouping students and addressing special considerations. The concepts and examples expressed in this chapter (and further detailed in chapters 4 and 5, pages 67 and 83) model how PCBE scheduling *can* be done, not how it *must* be done. This information is a guide for creating a scheduling system that fits the needs of your school or district. You should adapt each concept presented here depending on which variables apply to your particular situation; for instance, your district might have smaller or larger student populations, more or fewer educational levels within buildings, or more or fewer educators available.

Designing a PCBE Schedule

At this point, the school has gathered and analyzed the necessary data, identified each student's level of achievement in each content area, and grouped all its students accordingly. Now, the following question arises: What kind of schoolwide schedule will make the best use of the school's existing resources and allow decision makers to assign all students to classrooms that meet their needs?

Answering that question is not as simple as placing all the students in the school who have not yet completed seventh-grade mathematics standards in a class geared to teach those standards; there are a great many other considerations that the scheduling team needs to contemplate in deciding how classes and schedules are to be structured. In the following sections, we discuss several of these important considerations: horizontal and vertical schedules, length of class periods, interdisciplinary classes, and technology.

Horizontal and Vertical Schedules

The focus of this book is to help schools develop a master PCBE schedule. By *master schedule* we mean a schoolwide schedule that includes the who, the what, and the when of the school day. It essentially shows what, where, when, and to whom all the instructional staff members will be teaching. There are two main approaches to structuring a schoolwide PCBE schedule: (1) horizontal scheduling and (2) vertical scheduling. We discuss these two options in depth in chapters 4 and 5 (pages 67 and 83). Briefly, horizontal scheduling is the process of organizing students so they all engage in similar learning during the same period of the school day—for example, all students have English language arts (at their appropriate level) in the first period of the day, mathematics in the second period, and so on. Horizontal scheduling focuses on assigning one content area per class period, but it assumes educators are generalists and qualified to teach multiple content areas.

Figure 3.1 illustrates a simplified version of a horizontal schedule. The school day is broken up into five periods and each period is assigned to a specific content area; therefore all available educators are addressing the same content area simultaneously schoolwide. This greatly enhances the ability to initially group students according to academic needs, as well as increasing flexibility in regrouping students as their learning progresses throughout the year.

Vertical scheduling is more closely related to a traditional schedule and is often used in middle schools and high schools. Educators in these schools typically have narrower certifications, so there are fewer available to instruct each content area and grade level. Vertical scheduling addresses this problem by having educators teach multiple iterations of a course throughout the day, providing multiple time periods where students could receive that content area instruction. Students are placed in the classroom that is as closely aligned to their needs as possible. Because scheduling conflicts are more common in vertical scheduling, it is important for the scheduling team to prioritize content areas. The highest priority content area is placed in the schedule and students assigned to those classes first so it will have the fewest conflicts. Scheduling continues into other content areas; when conflicts arise, the team may have to assign students to classes that are a close but not perfect match for their needs. Thus, the potential range of student needs in a class increases with each consecutive content area added. Though it's not as flexible an approach as horizontal scheduling, vertical scheduling still improves on traditional age-based scheduling in that it reduces the range of student need within each classroom, especially for priority content areas.

Figure 3.2 illustrates a simplified version of a vertical schedule. The school day is still broken up into five periods, but the number of available educators to teach each content area is reduced to three.

	Teacher A	Teacher B	Teacher C	Teacher D	Teacher E	Teacher F	Teacher G	Teacher H	Teacher I	Teacher J	Teacher K	Teacher L	Teacher M	Teacher N	Teacher O
Period 1	ELA	ELA	ELA	ELA	ELA	ELA	ELA	ELA	ELA	ELA	ELA	ELA	ELA	ELA	ELA
Period 2	Mathematics	Mathematics	Mathematics	Mathematics	Mathematics	Mathematics	Mathematics	Mathematics	Mathematics	Mathematics	Mathematics	Mathematics	Mathematics	Mathematics	Mathematics
Period 3	Science	Science	Science	Science	Science	Science	Science	Science	Science	Science	Science	Science	Science	Science	Science
Lunch/Recess															
Period 4	Social Studies	Social Studies	Social Studies	Social Studies	Social Studies	Social Studies	Social Studies	Social Studies	Social Studies	Social Studies	Social Studies	Social Studies	Social Studies	Social Studies	Social Studies
Period 5	Electives	Electives	Electives	Electives	Electives	Electives	Electives	Electives	Electives	Electives	Electives	Electives	Electives	Electives	Electives

Figure 3.1: General example of a horizontal schedule.

	Teacher A	Teacher B	Teacher C	Teacher D	Teacher E	Teacher F	Teacher G	Teacher H	Teacher I	Teacher J	Teacher K	Teacher L	Teacher M	Teacher N	Teacher O
Period 1	ELA	ELA	ELA	Math	Math	Math	Science	Science	Science	Social Studies	Social Studies	Social Studies	Electives	Electives	Electives
Period 2	ELA	ELA	ELA	Math	Math	Math	Science	Science	Science	Social Studies	Social Studies	Social Studies	Electives	Electives	Electives
Period 3	ELA	ELA	ELA	Math	Math	Math	Science	Science	Science	Social Studies	Social Studies	Social Studies	Electives	Electives	Electives
Lunch/Recess															
Period 4	ELA	ELA	ELA	Math	Math	Math	Science	Science	Science	Social Studies	Social Studies	Social Studies	Electives	Electives	Electives
Period 5	ELA	ELA	ELA	Math	Math	Math	Science	Science	Science	Social Studies	Social Studies	Social Studies	Electives	Electives	Electives

Figure 3.2: General example of a vertical schedule.

Assume ELA has been chosen as the anchor content area, with students being most accurately grouped according to their ELA needs. Each successive content area added to the schedule would increase the probability of a wider range of student needs due to the reduced number of classroom options that works with each student's time availability. So, while a vertical schedule may look like a traditional one, it hides the fact that student data drives the grouping decisions, to the highest degree in anchor content areas.

In developing a PCBE schedule, administrators and teachers will have to determine which method might work best for the range of student needs present in their school—or they might determine a hybrid approach would be better. As mentioned above, often horizontal schedules would work better where there are more generalist educators with certifications that cover a range of content areas, as in many elementary school settings, and vertical schedules work better when there are educators with specific content area certifications, as in many middle and high schools. Developing horizontal and vertical schedules will be discussed in depth in chapters 4 and 5 (pages 67 and 83).

Length of Class Periods

A school's bell schedule (that is, the division of each school day into classes, blocks, or periods) is a factor in designing a PCBE schedule because it affects the number of classes available within a day and how the content areas are addressed throughout a week. Common bell schedules include block schedules and period schedules. A block schedule usually consists of four longer class sessions called *blocks*, with an alternating schedule throughout the week (meaning not every content area occurs every day). A traditional period schedule often involves six or seven classes per day, each about fifty minutes long.

Each school must look carefully at the overall pattern of needs among its student body and ask whether a six- or seven-period day or a four-block schedule works better for its PCBE system. The goal is to provide students the time and depth of content they need to meet content standards. Each option has positive and negative aspects; the question the scheduling team needs to ask is whether students will most benefit by having more periods to cover a broader range of content (period schedule) or by having more time per period to address a content area at a greater depth per session with fewer sessions per week, or to allow for cross-curricular opportunities like team teaching of multiple content areas within each extended time period (block schedule). This matter requires careful consideration; do not assume jumping from one schedule type to the other will be a magic bullet, fixing any issues within your school system: "Merely changing the school bell schedule will not guarantee better student performance" (Rettig, 1999).

The scheduling examples presented in chapters 4 and 5 (pages 67 and 83) use a six-period schedule to exemplify horizontal and vertical scheduling; the six-period schedule's similarity to a traditional system enables readers in all stages of PCBE implementation to grasp the complexity of the scheduling process.

Interdisciplinary Classes

This book primarily refers to traditional content-area courses—English language arts, mathematics, science, social studies, and so on—when demonstrating how to create different PCBE schedules. However, PCBE schedules do not require separate, distinct content areas. Schools can organize learning in a variety of interdisciplinary ways to motivate and engage students. Project-based learning (PBL) is one option. According to the National Education Association (n.d.):

> PBL is viewed as a model for classroom activity that shifts away from teacher-centered instruction and emphasizes student-centered projects. This model helps make learning relevant to students by establishing connections to life outside the classroom and by addressing real world issues.

Though there is flexibility within the projects, allowing students to follow a theme, their own personal interests, or probing questions that engage them throughout the process, PBL within PCBE is standards-based in design. All projects, explorations, and learning outcomes are tied back to standards, but instead of learning specific content-area topics in smaller chunks with assessments to prove proficiency, the projects incorporate a wider cross-curricular set of standards that students need to master, with the different stages or artifacts within the project design and completion process used as evidence of standards mastery. PBL instruction could be from generalist educators or from teams of content-area educators with the appropriate expertise.

Cross-curricular instruction or collaboration is not just for PBL, though, as schools might employ cross-curricular, team-taught classes that combine English language arts and social studies for example, or mathematics and science, but do not necessarily use projects as the basis for content delivery and mastery. Specialists who teach music, art, technology, physical education, and so on might be involved in a PBL setting to support student projects, or in a cross-curricular setting by collaborating with other content area teachers during a block period.

Some schools design their schedules so they blend traditional and interdisciplinary approaches, coupling traditional classes that expose students to standard content with at least one period of more flexible instructional time where students focus on their individual needs and interests. Marzano and colleagues (2017) refer to this flexible time as *power hour, advisory,* or *WIN (What I Need) time.* (Chapter 5, page 83, provides more information on power hour.) This schedule variant can also serve as a jumping-off point for schools to begin the transition to PCBE scheduling.

There are limitless ways to design learning within a PCBE system, so schools need not use traditional content areas as the sole focus for organizing a schedule.

Technology

Given the multitude of variables such as the number of students, certified educators, available locations, and so on involved in schedule creation, schools should consider using scheduling software to accelerate the process. Many school-scheduling programs are available. Some examples include PowerScheduler, Infinite Campus, Classter, Teach'n Go, and Sawyer, to name a few. These programs are designed to create traditional school schedules that accommodate many, but not necessarily all, of the variables associated with transitioning to a PCBE schedule.

When selecting one of these programs, PCBE schools must determine if the software allows for creating a schedule based on student learning need rather than age. They must ask, "Will the system allow us to input learning data so we can set class rosters by students' readiness level?" Additionally, "Will the system allow students to be working in a different levels across content areas?" Because age is no longer the main factor in organizing students within a schedule, schools (or rather, their scheduling teams working in conjunction with the IT departments) may need to develop creative tweaks within the scheduling system to accommodate the new variables. For example, the schedule might be broken down into smaller time increments in order to allow for more flexibility of student placement. Because PCBE scheduling uses grade-level data and specific standards data as the main pieces of information to organize students, those data need to be entered into the scheduling system. Working through the fine details of different scheduling systems is up to the schools and districts and will take some experimentation.

Once a school has designed its schedule by selecting from among the various options discussed here, it can begin the transition process.

Transitioning to a PCBE Schedule

The transition to a PCBE system from a traditional system is far more difficult than day-to-day teaching and learning in a fully implemented PCBE system. Though it will be worth the challenge, the shift to PCBE and a corresponding schedule will take time. Everyone involved—leaders, staff, students, and caregivers—needs to adjust.

Think of the transition as having two groups of students: we'll call the first group *today students* and the second group *tomorrow students*. Today students are the ones who are currently sitting in schools, learning in the traditional system. Today students, no matter which grade they are in, have worked within the traditional system throughout their entire educational careers, which affects them culturally—in the way they may view education as a passive endeavor about which they have little to no control—and academically—in the way current structures accept large learning gaps as normal and allow students to graduate with wildly variable sets of skills and knowledge. Today students may be struggling in one or more content areas and need extra time to learn grade-level standards. The old system does not allow for more time, so they have gotten low grades in those subjects. Except in the most extreme cases, they will move on to the next grade level anyway, each year's gaps compounding as today students fall further and further behind.

Tomorrow students are those who will experience a fully implemented PCBE system where learning gaps are actively avoided. They will all work at their own appropriate pace, completing each class or level only when they can demonstrate their proficiency on the standards. They will arrive in each subsequent level better prepared, allowing teachers to present more new content and use time more efficiently. The goal of transitioning to a PCBE system is to turn today students into tomorrow students.

If this sounds like a major effort, it should. Effective transitions can take anywhere from three to five years to complete. Those three to five years are the hardest years to work through because schools will expect today students to catch up and learn what tomorrow students would already know at the equivalent point in their education. Transitioning too quickly to a PCBE system or failing to make accommodations during the transition would require students with potentially large learning gaps (today students) to be proficient at all grade-level standards (tomorrow student expectations) to graduate, which is not realistic. The closer a student is to high school graduation, the more disruptive the transition can be, and therefore a single high school wishing to move toward PCBE might approach the transition much differently from a lower elementary school. A high school might take additional time to fully implement all aspects of PCBE scheduling, utilizing a slow phasing-in period starting with the lowest grade level.

School administrators and educators may find the first few years of transitioning to need-based scheduling difficult because the today students' learning gaps will quickly become apparent and may seem overwhelming. The best solution to that problem is for educators to focus on what students know and don't know in comparison to the standards for graduation. Even though the data may at first be disheartening, if a school utilizes a multiyear transition plan, creating a PCBE schedule will become easier as the school progresses through the transition process, as teachers will have more time to identify and fill academic gaps than just the first year of the transition. For more specifics on multiyear transition plans, please see *A Handbook for Personalized Competency-Based Education*, chapter 7: "How Do Schools and Districts Transition to a PCBE System?" (Marzano et al., 2017, p. 171).

Fine-Tuning the Initial PCBE Schedule

Once a school has established its initial PCBE schedule, the school should set up a buffer period which allows time to discover any errors in the schedule and student placements. Such errors occur for various reasons, ranging from mistakes in developing and using the comprehensive assessments, to students being distracted or tired during the test, to hidden biases affecting the assessment data's validity or reliability. During the buffer period, the teacher verifies whether students are actually ready for the range of content that he or she will present in a given class. If the teacher observes that a student is performing at a much higher or lower level than what his or her initial data suggested, then the student could be reassigned within the schedule to a more appropriate learning environment.

As student data become more robust and reliable over time, leading to more accurate student placement, schools will have less need for a buffer period. The buffer period, which initially may be several weeks (see How to Address Specific Standards Data, page 40), might be reduced to a few days. One exception is for transfer students; we address this topic later in this chapter (page 64).

Regrouping Students Within a PCBE Schedule

Schedulers face the question of when and how often to regroup students within a schedule. In a traditional system, students are typically *regrouped*, or assigned to new classes, at the start of a school year, semester, or term. For PCBE, there is no hard-and-fast rule about the time frame to regroup students because groupings are based on knowledge, not age or time. Whatever regrouping period is chosen might also include an additional buffer period of fine-tuning to catch any errors or transitional needs; for example, a student may have passed a level and been grouped into the next level of learning, but might either struggle with the new content or show evidence the new content is not challenging enough, so adjustments might be made. The further into the PCBE implementation process a school goes, the less likelihood there is of this being a common occurrence. The key takeaway is that any movement of students should be purposeful and improve their learning. If students' academic and behavioral data indicate the need for reorganization, and the school can create better learning environments by reorganizing, then regrouping should take place.

The type of schedule chosen might also affect regrouping timing and frequency, as horizontal schedules can be more responsive to changes since content areas are taught during the same time periods. Students can easily move to the next level whenever they reach mastery and not impact other areas of the schedule, whereas regrouping within vertical schedules is more interconnected and impacts the whole. Generally speaking, though, the most common and logical time to regroup students is still at the start of a new quarter or semester, if quarters and semesters continue to be a part of the school calendar, keeping in mind that student mastery is not time bound and educators still need to instruct students according to their needs.

Schedulers must think about the frequency at which regrouping should occur. One might assume that flexible PCBE scheduling means that students are continually moving into new classes to match their changing proficiency level, but this is not necessarily the case. Frequent regrouping should *not* be a common practice for a few reasons. First, frequently changing groups assumes that all groups frequently have need of change, which is rarely the case after a PCBE schedule has been initially established. More often it may be just a handful of groups that have such student pacing differences that the span of content being covered has become so large as to need immediate regrouping. Second, due to the interrelated nature of schedules (especially vertical schedules), any regrouping choices impact many if not all areas of the schedule, so frequent regrouping would require major reworking of the entire schedule over and over, which is not realistic due to the time and effort needed. Third, frequent shuffling is disruptive to the culture of the school and classrooms. Obviously, if students move in and out of classrooms every few weeks, it is harder for teachers to establish consistent procedures and positive relationships. Finally, frequent regrouping should not be necessary if schools group students accurately. Since PCBE scheduling places students in a class that will address the set of standards they all need to learn, pacing differences—much smaller than the five grade levels within one age-based classroom—can be managed by small-group instruction targeted to need rather than a disruptive move to another classroom. The few students who might need to move are outliers and can be dealt with on a case-by-case basis.

With all this in mind, even if a school utilizes a specific time period for regrouping within the school year, such as every semester, this does not mean that a systemwide regrouping would always have to happen. It means that during that period, educators analyze the most recent standards-based student data to ensure that the current grouping *still reflects* the best situations for student learning. This is a check-and-adjust period to keep decisions around scheduling tied to the most accurate and up-to-date student data. If the data show that many groups are seeing increasing spreads of learning needs and pacing differences that are becoming unwieldly to address within classrooms, it would make sense to address regrouping schoolwide.

Again, there are differences within vertical schedules and horizontal schedules in the amount of impact a change has on the rest of the schedule. Schools with horizontal schedules and greater flexibility may adopt a model that involves, for example, a protocol of student transition to another classroom rather than a specific time period of transition that might be adopted by schools with vertical schedules.

Addressing Special Considerations in the PCBE Scheduling Process

Scheduling in PCBE is essentially just organizing students based on similar needs so more efficient, focused instruction and learning can occur. Transitioning to a PCBE system does, however, require that schools also consider how to address specialized needs and IEPs, how to incorporate structures designed for the traditional system (such as standardized tests and teacher certifications), how to best place students whose learning needs do not fall neatly into one level, and how to assimilate transfer students into the PCBE system.

Individualized Education Plans

Within special education, IEPs support students with disabilities so they can be successful with public education. IEPs can be written with *accommodations*, which means that the students have the same learning requirements but with the aid of strategies, tools, and procedures to support learning. IEPs can also be written with *modifications*, which means that the actual learning requirements are altered to adapt to the students' abilities while also incorporating strategies, tools, and procedures (Office of Special Education Programs, n.d.).

In either case, IEPs clarify the learning expectations and dictate what classes or groups students can be assigned to. If an IEP dictates that a student is expected to be in a certain age group and be presented certain content, then that is what needs to occur within the PCBE schedule. For example, if the IEP requires access to grade-level content but the student is so far below grade level that grouping them according to need would not support having access to grade-level content, the student would be grouped according the requirements of the IEP. Often students with high-level needs like this have additional supports such as push-in support with a paraprofessional or special education teacher supporting them in their classroom or pull-out instruction in a separate classroom to get targeted instruction or support, which helps to ensure their learning progress. PCBE does not supersede the objectives of an IEP, but much of the PCBE approach and its understanding of students and variable rates of learning aligns with special education beliefs and processes. PCBE is about individualizing education for all students, not just students with special needs.

Standardized Testing

Standardized testing is a reality of life in modern education. Creating a PCBE schedule and fully implementing a PCBE system require a unique approach to prepare students for age-based standardized assessments. With the PCBE approach's focus on identifying learning gaps, filling those gaps, and providing students with an appropriate pace for learning, a student may or may not get direct contact with the standards that will be on the age-based assessment in a certain academic year. Individual needs will dictate what students learn, so students will have various levels of exposure to the grade-level standards.

It takes time to fill in the learning gaps left by the traditional system, so schools or districts moving to PCBE might not see immediate increase in test scores. But over several years, results will stabilize and improve as mastery requirements take hold. For example, Westminster Public Schools (WPS) in Westminster, Colorado, began their shift to competency-based education in the early 2000s and have steadily deepened their work and commitment to this change. In 2019, their state test data showed three consecutive years of "sustained growth was across the board, including in the following categories: All Students, English Language Learners, Free and Reduced Lunch Students, Students with Individual Education Plans (IEP), and Minority Students." In general, "for the fourth consecutive year, elementary and middle school students . . . showed an increase in academic achievement in both English Language Arts and Math" (Westminster Public Schools, 2019b). In addition, graduation rates have risen exponentially, from 60.5 percent in 2012 to 81.9 percent in 2019 (Westminster Public Schools, 2013, 2019a). These statistics are impressive on their face but understanding the time, commitment, and work behind these numbers is very important. In other words, districts or schools should not expect that moving toward PCBE is a quick or easy way to increase standardized test scores.

So, while PCBE schedules don't specifically focus on achieving greater success on one particular grade-level standardized test, they allow students to move from level to level with fewer to no academic gaps, which allows for greater learning success overall. Instruction targeted to need is also much more efficient, and students who are below grade level get only what they are missing and can increase pacing to come closer to age-based grade-level content more quickly, which ultimately improves their performance on age-based standardized tests.

Teacher Certification

The fact that students of different ages will receive the same instruction in the same classroom may raise concerns around teacher certification, which is a variable that affects the success of a PCBE schedule. The certification process normally assumes that an individual's certification range is also connected to a certain age range. If a teacher is certified to teach seventh- and eighth-grade science, then some people assume that they can only teach students in the age range traditionally assigned to seventh and eighth grade—that is, 11.9 to 13.8 years old. Working in a PCBE system questions that assumption because younger or older students can be given the opportunity to learn seventh-grade content.

If a sixth-grade-aged student needs seventh-grade science content, then a teacher specifically certified for seventh- and eighth-grade science is qualified to teach that student even though the student is not of seventh-grade age—the certification is connected to the content and not the student's age. If a ninth-grade-aged student needs eighth-grade science content, then again, the seventh- and eighth-grade science certification qualifies the teacher to teach that student because the instruction is within the certification area of middle school science.

Challenges arise in the traditional schedule when a seventh-grade-aged student needs fifth-grade science content or an eighth-grade-aged student needs high school science content. Is a certified seventh- and eighth-grade science teacher qualified to teach the fifth- and ninth-grade content? We would argue that yes, this teacher is certainly capable of addressing lower- or higher-level content and, in fact, educators are doing this in traditional classrooms everywhere when they review content from previous grades levels or challenge students with above-grade-level content. In a PCBE system, student learning needs are the driver—so teacher certification is much less of a hindrance to scheduling, but some issues can arise. For example, if schoolwide data show that a large number of students require lower-grade-level content at a certification cusp, then many staff would be teaching outside their certifications. For example, if many students in a middle school need to learn fourth- and fifth-grade content, teachers certified for grades 6–8 would be teaching outside their certifications.

Another issue is teacher willingness or perception. Though it is not the norm, there are teachers who feel more connected with their specific yearly content-area expectations than to individual student needs. They identify themselves with, say, teaching sixth-grade mathematics, and would be averse to teaching lower- or higher-grade-level content. In these examples, schools will have to think creatively about student grouping, placement, labeling, and shifting mindsets. All content area standards have deep connections throughout the grade levels, so even as one grade level might be the specific focus, there are certainly many ways PCBE scheduling can be considered remediation or advanced placement when students work outside their age-based expectations. These certification issues are relatively minor and shouldn't stop schools from adopting a PCBE schedule.

One real challenge with teacher certification is when middle or high schools want to design a horizontal PCBE schedule, which requires more teachers to have multiple content area certifications, similar to an elementary generalist. In horizontal scheduling, all educators address the same content area at the same time so students can be placed in whatever class is most aligned with their learning needs. Having a general K–8 certification, which some states offer, allows for the largest range of freedom of instruction. This alleviates many issues with assigning teachers to certain levels within a content area. Since elementary educators are typically certified as generalists, their certifications work well for creating a horizontal or vertical PCBE schedule. If all the teachers in an elementary school are K–8 certified, anyone can teach any content area and grade level that the students are likely to need, making scheduling easier. An elementary school where the teachers have narrower certifications (for example, K–2, 3–5, and 6–8) must pay more attention when scheduling classes to make sure teachers are delivering content within their area of certification.

Middle schools (usually grades 6–8) and junior high schools (grades 7–9) vary depending on how the certification process is organized in a state or province. Some schools have K–8 generalist teachers, others intermediate generalist teachers, and still others content-area certified teachers. The first two situations are similar to elementary schools and do not create any major issues. In the third situation, where teachers are certified in a certain content area, the approach to PCBE scheduling will be more like the high school scheduling process.

In high schools, teachers are usually certified in specific content areas. That makes it difficult to create a horizontal schedule; most PCBE high schools will adopt vertical scheduling. Also, content areas in high school are less tied to age-based grade levels than content areas in elementary and middle school. A mathematics teacher might have a specific certification in a particular area of mathematics, such as geometry (which students in any grade might take), rather than a particular grade. The PCBE scheduling process for high school is constrained by the number of classes available within a certain class period due to these teacher certifications. In a high school, there may be only five teachers certified to instruct a certain content area, such as chemistry, so that limits the number of classes available. Until the larger issue of narrow certification is addressed at the state or provincial level, teacher certification will mostly likely dictate that PCBE middle and high schools adopt a vertical schedule. But we challenge schools and districts to push into this area and find creative solutions to this problem. For example, with mentor teacher support, a team-teaching, multidisciplinary approach within a block schedule addresses many of the certification issues.

Students Who Are Working Within Multiple Grade Levels

During the process of establishing grade-level data and specific standards data, there will be situations in which some students actually know a few standards in one grade level and a few standards in another grade level of the same content area, an unfortunate byproduct of the traditional system, where gaps develop in students' learning. In the process of shifting to a PCBE system, the school identifies such gaps and focuses on specifically reducing them. This gap identification at the initial transition is a temporary problem because once students move through a fully implemented PCBE system, reaching proficiency on all standards is a requirement to prevent gaps from forming. That does not mean that every student progresses at the same pace; it just means that content is not skipped over simply because the teacher is required to cover the age-based material within a certain time period.

Within a PCBE system, the fundamental component of allowing students to work at their appropriate pace can cause a student to be working in multiple levels of content at the same time. For example, within the content area of mathematics, a sixth-grade-aged student may be advanced at geometry standards and desire to keep moving through the upper grade levels of geometry. If given the opportunity, this student may move through multiple levels of geometry above their age-based grade level but still be struggling in the sixth-grade-level standards for algebraic expressions. Schools must balance these needs so that they give students opportunities to learn at their appropriate pace but also guide them in completing all the grade-level expectations and working on areas of need. There needs to be a balance in affording choice and ensuring grade-level completion in an efficient, effective way.

A general rule of thumb is for a student to stay within two consecutive grade levels—meaning that a student could be working in seventh-grade-level geometry and also working on other sixth-grade-level mathematics standards. We do not recommend that the student work on sixth-grade, seventh-grade, and eighth-grade standards at the same time. Once the student completes all the sixth-grade-level standards and moves up to the seventh-grade-level standards, then the eighth-grade standards can be opened up for the student to learn. This can also serve as motivation for students to learn all the standards in a grade level because they want to continue with the areas they excel at and enjoy more.

Some may think that limiting students' learning to two consecutive grade levels goes against the foundational definition of PCBE (students working at their own pace), or even that two consecutive grade levels is too much and students should have to complete all grade-level standards before starting on the next level. But we believe this compromise creates a manageable, appropriate system that allows for both flexibility and structure. We encourage school sites to find their own systems for addressing these two aspects of PCBE that work for them and their students. There is always a balancing act going on within PCBE, and this area is no different.

Transfer Students

Students are forever transferring from one school to the next. This part of life is unavoidable, so schools need to develop a procedure to deal with new students. Fortunately, a school district that has already transitioned to a PCBE system has conducted all the necessary steps to get a new student ready for a PCBE learning environment. Remember, at one time, all the current students were effectively transferring to PCBE. After the initial leveling, the process for determining grade-level data and specific standards data only needs to be conducted for transfer students.

A transfer student arrives with a traditional transcript, which rarely gives specific standards-based data about what a student knows and does not know. The transcript may address the general areas of what a student has achieved, and it can provide guidance in determining which comprehensive assessments the student needs to take. If a student has an A or B in seventh-grade mathematics, then he or she should take the seventh-grade comprehensive assessment to determine his or her precise knowledge. If a student has a C or D in seventh-grade mathematics, then testing may start with the sixth-grade assessment, as the school needs information about the student's last level of proficiency. The traditional grades on transfer students' transcripts provide the starting point for which assessments a school should give to the students to determine the best groups for learning. The PCBE school has already gone through the entire process of creating each grade-level assessment, and the school must keep and organize all the comprehensive assessments to develop the transfer-student process.

As an example, a PCBE school's transfer-student process might initially place transfer students according to age so they can learn the cultural components of PCBE—such as the school and class visions, behavioral expectations, and standard operating procedures—in a familiar setting (Marzano et al., 2017). During those first few days of school, the transfer students take comprehensive assessments based on their transcripts, and the results dictate the best academic placements. The school should use all available behavioral data as a filter for placement if necessary. With this large amount of up-front testing, transfer-student processes need to have a buffer time to correct any errors from the comprehensive test results, just as the initial comprehensive data process used to place all current students in the PCBE system had.

Summary

Scheduling in a PCBE system focuses on different variables than scheduling in a traditional system does. Student data drive the process, and classes are organized by what students need to learn. Teachers are tasked with addressing those needs and providing an appropriate pace for learning. In this chapter, we introduced two types of PCBE scheduling: (1) horizontal and (2) vertical. Horizontal scheduling is the process of assigning all classes on a particular content area to the same period within the school day. Vertical scheduling is the process of selecting an anchor subject area, such as mathematics; determining how many locations and qualified teachers are available throughout the day to address that content area; and then using student data to place the students. In determining how to develop the PCBE schedule, administrators and educators must examine the overall student needs and identify which schedule type will work better, or if a hybrid might be the best option. The transition from traditional to PCBE scheduling is challenging, and schools should expect it to take three to five years. The initial years will be hardest, as students with significant gaps who are nearing graduation will need intensive support to reach the graduation standards. As the transition process proceeds, the school's ability to reduce the impact of time restrictions on student learning will grow.

In the next chapter, we take a close look at horizontal schedules and the process of creating them.

Chapter 4

Creation of a Horizontal PCBE Schedule

I like keeping track of my learning so I can look back and see how I've done, and I can work harder and study more so I can do even better.

—Third-grade student

Horizontal scheduling refers to the process of organizing similar learning across the same class period. *Similar learning* can refer to either traditional subject-area courses or cross-curricular opportunities, such as project-based learning or interdisciplinary classes. In a school with a horizontal PCBE schedule, all or most students will be engaged with the same content area (at their appropriate levels) at a given point in the school day. In a broad example of a content-centered horizontal schedule, all students attend their mathematics classes during the second period of the day. During second period, all students are assigned to a classroom and a teacher according to what their data show about their learning needs in mathematics. This arrangement of one content area per class period across the entire school allows the most flexibility in the placement of students based on the standards they need to learn.

The advantage to horizontal scheduling is that it isolates subject areas from each other, which reduces the occurrence of scheduling conflicts when placing students in various classes. When all classes of one content area are scheduled during the same period, it dramatically reduces schedulers' inability to place students in the correct classes based on their needs. Horizontal scheduling all but solves the problem of a student's being assigned to a class that does not fit the individual's learning needs because the more appropriate class conflicts with another in the student's schedule. Further, when a student advances to the next level in a content area, movement to a different class can happen without disrupting the rest of the student's class schedule.

Creating a master schedule where, for instance, all students have English first period, mathematics second period, science third period, social studies fourth period, and so on would be ideal for student learning—but it may be unrealistic in a given school's real-world conditions, such as the teacher certification issues addressed in the previous chapter (page 61). Other issues such as bus schedules, lunch time, electives, prep periods, and the physical restraints of the school itself all affect the scheduling process. Most schools' facilities and equipment were designed with the understanding that age-based groups of students would rotate throughout the day. A perfectly horizontal PCBE schedule eliminates that rotation such that the school may not have enough equipment or facilities to allow all students who need them to use them at the same time, particularly if the school is under significant budget pressure or underserved in other ways. For example, a school's cafeteria may not have the capacity for the entire student body to eat lunch at the same time. Similarly, if all students in the school are to participate in science classes during the same period of the day, the school will need to have sufficient lab classrooms and equipment to serve all students at once.

The physical capacity of the school's spaces and equipment is one of many factors that may prevent the ideal horizontal schedule; others include teacher preparation periods, specials or electives, lunch periods, bus schedules, and special education requirements, just to name a few. To create a real-world (more feasible) horizontal schedule, schedulers may establish one or two periods of schoolwide instruction in particular content areas and then adjust each successive class period to address different variables. This means that the available classes in those remaining periods may not all be devoted to a single content area. For example, the scheduling team might decide to have fully horizontal classes for English and mathematics during the first two periods of the day but then divide the students into three subgroups, so that in period 3, some students have lunch, others have physical education or recess, and the third group has science—due to their school's limited facilities for science exploration. The subgroups then rotate in periods 4 and 5. This ensures all students can access the content area with limited facilities, as well as lunch and phys ed—but it also has inherent challenges associated with appropriately grouping students to meet their individual learning needs in science. Figure 4.1 compares a sample real-world horizontal schedule to the ideal. In this example, all students have a homeroom and warm-up class during first period and attend their appropriate level course for the school's priority content area during second period. For third, fourth, and fifth periods, students rotate through areas with limited resources, and the day concludes with all students taking an elective or lower-priority content course during sixth period.

Teacher certifications can also be a limiting factor for horizontal scheduling. As mentioned in chapter 3 (page 61), elementary schools that have generalist teacher certifications that span a wide grade-level range are ideal for horizontal scheduling. Middle schools that have similar certifications also fall into this category. Broad teacher certification makes more teachers available to instruct in particular content areas within the same class periods—if all teachers are generalists, they are all available to teach science during first period, for example, which is not the case when teachers have content-specific certifications or a narrow range of grade-level certifications such as early elementary (K–2) or middle school (6–8) certifications.

Horizontal Scheduling: Ideal Situation

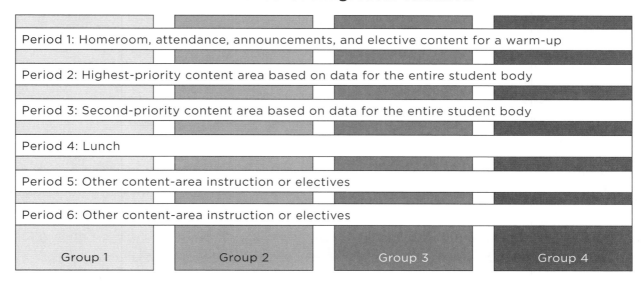

Horizontal Scheduling: Real-World Situation Where Facilities Are Limited

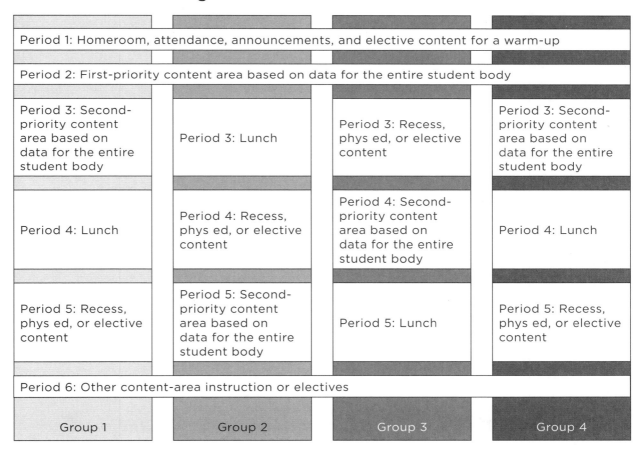

Figure 4.1: Ideal and real-world horizontal schedules.

For high schools and for middle schools that are designed like high schools, horizontal scheduling is more difficult to achieve. Their course design and teacher certifications mean that the schools may not have the human resources needed to teach a single content area to all students during one class period. A vertical schedule or an adapted horizontal schedule is a more realistic approach for these schools. As mentioned in chapter 3 (Teacher Certification, page 61), schools wishing to attempt this schedule type have to overcome obstacles that prevent educators from addressing content areas besides their own. Schools may think creatively about pairing or grouping teachers with multiple content area expertise and adopting a team-teaching approach, but this also assumes that the physical layout allows for larger class sizes. Another opportunity available to modern education is through technology. Students can learn from a certified teacher in another school or another state, virtually, with support available from staff members on site. Additionally, with 360-degree camera technology or a simple recording device on a tripod, a school site could record all instruction in all classrooms in the year prior to the full transition and create virtual lessons for all content areas from the site-based educators.

There are four main steps to creating a horizontal PCBE schedule.

1. Establishing the foundation for scheduling
2. Organizing students for the initial class period
3. Assigning teachers to classes
4. Adding more content areas and class periods

The following sections delineate each step.

Establishing the Foundation for Scheduling

There are a few key questions that the scheduling team need to answer before setting up a horizontal schedule. Those questions include:

- During which class period should we start horizontal scheduling?
- In what content area should we start horizontal scheduling?
- How many classes can be formed in the chosen period?

The answers to these questions set the foundation for the schedule and absolutely must be determined before analyzing the grade-level data and specific standards data to group students.

During Which Class Period Should We Start Horizontal Scheduling?

To begin crafting a horizontal PCBE schedule, schools should start with one class period dedicated to one content area. The first step is to select one period of the day to prioritize in the schedule.

Cognitive fatigue can occur later in the day and cause students to struggle, so it makes sense to begin the process for horizontal scheduling with an earlier class period (Sievertsen, Gino, & Piovesan 2016). As we develop a sample schedule in this chapter, we will focus on second period.

Other factors to keep in mind when determining which period to start with are the specials or electives schedules, lunch schedules, and teacher prep periods. The goal is to eliminate or at least limit those factors during at least one class period to start. Thus, avoid selecting a lunch period as the initial class period. Designate the initial class period as off-limits for electives and teacher prep periods that you will schedule later in the process. In our example, if electives, such as art, drama, music, band, and so on, were to be scheduled during second period, it would disrupt the focus on having one content area for all students.

In What Content Area Should We Start Horizontal Scheduling?

The next step is to select the content area that will be scheduled in the initial class period. As the first subject area entered into the horizontal schedule, it will have the least number of conflicts and variables to address. For our example, we will select English language arts as the initial content area and assign it to second period. Schedulers should use their school's academic data to decide which content area will anchor the horizontal schedule (that is, which content area receives priority and is scheduled first). Analyzing state test scores, district test scores, and individual student data will help determine the most critical area of need. So, scheduling starts by prioritizing the content area in which students have the greatest learning needs.

For instance, if the data show that students have significant learning gaps in English language arts, then ELA should be the anchor for the upcoming horizontal schedule. If mathematics is second to ELA in terms of knowledge gaps, then place mathematics in the schedule next. As other necessary variables are added in, the schedule becomes less universally aligned—that is part of the nature of the challenge, but overall, it will produce a more effective schedule for meeting student needs than the traditional version. Data-informed prioritization provides the best opportunity for students to receive targeted instruction in the content-area standards that they need. It creates the best opportunity to get students caught up in the priority content because it will make the groupings the most aligned and instruction the most efficient.

Once schools have emerged from the transitional period, scheduling should be a great deal easier, as the schools will have fewer gaps to fill in for all students. Schools will have less need to identify priority content areas, as students will be moving through grade-level standards at their own pace and will need less in the way of intensive informational backfilling to reach proficiency in all the required standards. While a school may use state testing data to drive its initial decisions around what content area to prioritize, the most updated standards-based student data (in addition to state testing data) would drive yearly content area prioritization for PCBE schools.

How Many Classes Can Be Formed in the Chosen Period?

With the class period (in our example, second period) and anchor content area (in this instance, ELA) established, the next step of setting a horizontal schedule's foundation is determining how many classes can be formed. This number is very important because it dictates into how many groups the whole student population needs to be organized. Two factors that come into play here are the number of available locations and the number of available teachers who are appropriately experienced and certified. These numbers govern how many classes a school can create within a period. Returning to our example middle school, imagine there are twenty available classrooms for second period. The school's twenty teachers have K–8 generalist certifications, so they can provide instruction on all the main content areas, including ELA.

To summarize our example thus far, we've selected second period as the initial class period and ELA as the anchor content area. Twenty classroom teachers is the limit to the number of groups that can form within second period. The next step is to organize the middle school's students into twenty ELA classes based on grade-level data and specific standards data.

Organizing Students for the Initial Class Period

The process of organizing students into classes for the anchor content area starts with analyzing the grade-level data for that subject. The example middle school placing ELA within second period analyzes the ELA grade-level data for the entire school. Table 4.1 shows the grade-level data of how the five hundred students are distributed across the grade levels and subcategories. The twenty classrooms and teachers available during second period are the main variables that drive the process of organizing these students.

Table 4.1: Current Grade-Level Data for All Middle School Students in ELA

FOURTH GRADE	FIFTH GRADE	BEGINNING OF SIXTH GRADE	MIDDLE OF SIXTH GRADE	BEGINNING OF SEVENTH GRADE	MIDDLE OF SEVENTH GRADE	BEGINNING OF EIGHTH GRADE	MIDDLE OF EIGHTH GRADE	BEGINNING OF NINTH GRADE	MIDDLE OF NINTH GRADE	BEGINNING OF TENTH GRADE	MIDDLE OF TENTH GRADE
30	111	83	63	87	50	50	12	9	2	3	0

The next step is to divide the number of students in each subcategory into classes. With five hundred students and twenty teachers, the average class size will be twenty-five. The school's scheduling team takes each subcategory and divides the number of students by twenty-five to determine the approximate number of classes per level, keeping in mind that the school can have only twenty ELA classes in total. Table 4.2 shows this step. Its Number of Groups row illustrates how the subcategories can be distributed while only creating those twenty classes.

Table 4.2: Sample Class Groupings for All Middle School Students in ELA

	FOURTH GRADE	FIFTH GRADE	SIXTH GRADE BEGINNING	SIXTH GRADE MIDDLE	SEVENTH GRADE BEGINNING	SEVENTH GRADE MIDDLE	EIGHTH GRADE BEGINNING	EIGHTH GRADE MIDDLE	NINTH GRADE BEGINNING	NINTH GRADE MIDDLE	BEGINNING OF TENTH GRADE
Total Number of Students per ELA Level	30	111	83	63	87	50	50	12	9	2	3
Number of Groups	2	4	3	3	3	2	2	1			
Number of Students per Group	15	≤ 28	≤ 28	21	29	25	25	26			

The class sizes range from fifteen students to twenty-nine students. It would be ideal to maintain a consistent twenty-five-to-one ratio, but the student data guide the process, and these data do not perfectly align with this ratio, as is often the case in real-world scheduling. Thus, schedulers will have to make decisions about smaller and larger class sizes.

As shown in table 4.2, thirty students need to learn fourth-grade content. These students have large learning gaps from the traditional system or perhaps learn ELA content at a slower pace. Knowing that these students are facing the greatest academic challenges, the school's schedulers determine these students would best learn in two classes of fifteen, rather than one class of thirty. Student achievement and engagement increase with smaller class sizes, most significantly for academically and behaviorally at-risk students (Blatchford, Bassett, & Brown, 2011).

At the other end of the data table, there is a class of twenty-six students ranging from the middle of eighth grade to the beginning of tenth grade. That range of academic content may dictate more opportunities for independent and small-group instruction and work, which can require more management. This class would be a priority to receive support services that facilitate independent learning, such as aides or instructional resources, because its students have such a wide range of learning needs.

In an alternate scenario, perhaps the schedulers determine that the middle of eighth grade through the beginning of tenth grade is too wide a range for one class. To avoid this, they redistribute the classes, making an adjustment from having two classes of fifteen students for the fourth-grade content group to having just one of thirty students. This new class has more students than desired, but its content range is within one grade level and therefore much easier to instruct. The scheduling team then adds a class for the twenty-six students working on middle-of-eighth-grade through beginning-of-tenth-grade content; they break up the twenty-six students into a group of twelve covering just the middle-of-eighth-grade content and a group of fourteen addressing ninth- and tenth-grade content. This alternate grouping reduces the range of content within the classes. Table 4.3 shows this alternate grouping.

Table 4.3: Alternate Class Groupings for All Middle School Students in ELA

	FOURTH GRADE	FIFTH GRADE	SIXTH GRADE		SEVENTH GRADE		EIGHTH GRADE		NINTH GRADE		BEGINNING OF TENTH GRADE
			BEGINNING	MIDDLE	BEGINNING	MIDDLE	BEGINNING	MIDDLE	BEGINNING	MIDDLE	
Total Number of Students per ELA Level	30	111	83	63	87	50	50	12	9	2	3
Number of Groups	1	4	3	3	3	2	2	1	1		
Number of Students per Group	30	≤ 28	≤ 28	21	29	25	25	12	14		

Though this second scenario is certainly an option, the initial scenario is preferable, keeping in mind the research on struggling students and smaller class sizes. So, if the schedulers choose the second scenario, they should do so with the caveat that they must give the class of thirty priority when assigning a highly effective teacher, as well as additional support staff and resources to address the learners' needs.

Using just the grade-level data, we have established the number of classes necessary to cover the range of needs for each subcategory. Next, schedulers need to assign students to the newly created classes. This is the time to reference the master list of students associated with the grade-level data. As stated in chapter 2 (page 21), when the grade-level data were collected, a corresponding master list of students in each subcategory was also created. The master list says which students are in which subcategory of the grade-level data.

Take the beginning-of-sixth-grade subcategory as an example of how schedulers assign students to classes. The schedulers determined the eighty-three students in that subcategory need to be organized into three classes with rosters of approximately twenty-seven students, twenty-eight students, and twenty-eight students. Although all these students are at approximately the same place in their learning (specifically, the beginning of sixth grade), schedulers should group the students based on their specific standards data, rather than at random. Analyzing the students' specific standards data will reveal patterns of similar needs within the standards. For example, some students may need to fill a few small gaps in the fifth-grade standards, and some may already be proficient on a few sixth-grade standards. Those students with similar needs would be placed into a class together. The first of the three classes may focus on filling fifth-grade content gaps and then moving to sixth-grade content, the second may start with beginning-of-sixth-grade content because its students are proficient in all fifth-grade standards and no sixth-grade standards, and the third may start ahead because the students already know some of the sixth-grade standards.

No matter how the students are organized within the three classes, the classes will have a potential range of needs that span less than a year of a content area expectations—whether that falls within one grade level or spans multiple levels (as in the class that will address some fifth-grade standards and then move to sixth-grade content). This is much more instructionally focused than the five-grade-level span common in traditional systems that chapter 1 mentioned (page 5; Firmender et al., 2012). Such a narrow range of learning needs is the ultimate goal for creating a PCBE schedule. It creates a learning environment that better supports the students and a teaching situation that is much more manageable and effective.

As stated previously (page 57), schools should start with academic data to make student placements and then consider behavioral information to make slight alterations to fit students' needs. Most students' placements will not need to be filtered through the behavioral data because a majority of students do not have behavioral issues that warrant special placement. On occasion, age might be a factor—that is, schedulers might purposefully place students of similar ages in the same class if their academic needs are the same. Whenever possible, reducing variables such as behavior, age span, social-emotional readiness, and so on is preferable unless it interferes with creating an appropriate learning environment for a student.

Assigning Teachers to Classes

Now that classes for the anchor content area are organized around the students' needs, it is time to assign teachers to all the classes during the initial class period. For our example, because all teachers in the school have K–8 generalist certifications, there are technically no restrictions on which teachers we can assign to which classes. However, it makes sense to assign teachers who have experience with certain grade-level content to the classes that need to cover that content. A possible approach would be to distribute the teachers who normally cover sixth-grade content throughout the fourth-, fifth-, and beginning-of-sixth-grade classes. Teachers who usually cover seventh grade would be assigned to the middle of sixth to the beginning of eighth grade, and teachers of eighth-grade content would be assigned to the beginning of eighth grade up to tenth grade.

The distribution of the classes dictates how many teachers will cover certain grade-level content. In this example, there is substantial need at lower grade levels—even though this is a middle school, nine classes (and thus nine teachers) need to cover fourth-, fifth-, and beginning-of-sixth-grade content. This means that many teachers in the school will end up teaching lower-grade-level content than they would have in the traditional system. Some sixth-grade teachers will teach fourth- and fifth-grade content, potentially creating a shortage at the sixth-grade level. To solve this, some seventh-grade teachers would then be assigned to sixth-grade content, and some eighth-grade teachers to seventh-grade content. How this shift occurs is up to the specific schools and districts. The student data dictate the needs, and the system has to be flexible and responsive to address those needs.

When it comes to teaching higher-grade-level content, schools may have to be creative. Access to teacher resources and student resources is the biggest issue. A middle school such as the one in our example may or may not have an educator on staff who can provide effective instruction in ninth- and tenth-grade content. If no one on staff can teach the higher-level content, numerous solutions are available. Depending on the physical location of the middle school in relation to the high school, students might travel to the high school for upper-level courses. Also, high school teachers could provide instruction for distance-learning opportunities, with the middle school teachers or paraprofessionals giving on-site supervision and support. The main goal of these solutions is to allow the students access to upper-grade content and instruction in the best environment possible, within the district's available options.

Individual educators' abilities and strengths are also a factor in class assignments. Placing highly effective educators—those who, based on data, have the greatest positive impact on student achievement—with groups of struggling learners would have the most positive effect on those students. Research by William L. Sanders and June C. Rivers (1996) and the Tennessee Department of Education Division of Data and Research (2016) found that while all students benefit by having highly effective teachers, those who are the most at risk in their learning benefit most significantly from highly effective teachers and have the greatest need for them. Too often, struggling learners have the least access to quality education, which is exactly what the Research and Data team (Tennessee Department of Education, 2016) found during its statewide analysis. So, whenever possible, placing students who have the most significant achievement gaps in smaller classes with highly effective educators will close those gaps the fastest and give those students the most supportive environment in which to flourish.

In a class with a wide range of content levels (such as the middle-of-eighth-grade through beginning-of-tenth-grade class from our example), an educator needs a specific set of skills. The educator assigned to this type of class needs strong classroom management skills and the ability to support the development of student agency, more than efficacy in delivering content. Because classes with a wide range of content levels are more likely to occur in above-grade-level subcategories, the educator also needs the content-area expertise to assist students in learning above-grade-level standards.

Adding More Content Areas and Class Periods

Once the scheduling team sets a schedule for the initial class period, they can assign content areas to the remaining class periods. The more class periods that they horizontally schedule, the better the overall schedule will address students' learning needs, and the more it will reduce the range of content that a teacher has to cover within each classroom. As more class periods are added into the schedule, however, more variables arise. Teachers need prep periods. Students must eat lunch. Electives are a crucial component to a good education. Subsequently, the scheduling team has less ability to assign one content area per period. In some cases, schools design two or three class periods as a horizontal schedule, and then they schedule the remaining class periods more traditionally to accommodate the variables throughout a school day. All stakeholders need to be open to alternate plans and ways of thinking, as compromise and adaptation to real-life variables are necessary in this process, and creative problem solvers have more success than people with a fixed mindset. However, the anchor subject is set in the schedule, and schools should make every effort to leave that alone.

In our example middle school, now that ELA has been established as second period, the scheduling team next moves to the other content areas. The same process that occurred for ELA occurs for all the other content areas. Remember the three foundational questions: (1) During which class period should we start horizontal scheduling? (2) In what content area should we start horizontal scheduling? (3) How many classes can be formed within the chosen class period? The scheduling team now modifies these questions to ask which class period and content area they should address next. Through discussions and needs analyses for specials or electives, prep periods, and subject-area data—keeping in mind the bounds created by the physical layout as well as any other physical or human resources available—the team determines that third period has the least variables to add, so they decide they will next schedule this period. They select mathematics as the next-priority content area based on school data.

The scheduling team uses the grade-level mathematics data and teacher-student ratio to determine the number of classes needed for each subcategory. The master list of student names associated with the grade-level data and the specific standards data guide which students the team will locate in each classroom. They also look for similarities in the specific standards data to group the students accordingly. Before assigning students and teachers to specific classes, they identify the number of classes per subcategory and the size of each class. See tables 4.4 (page 78), 4.5 (page 78), and 4.6 (page 79) for samples of this breakdown for mathematics, science, and social studies in our example middle school.

Table 4.4: Sample Class Groupings for All Middle School Students in Mathematics

	FOURTH GRADE	FIFTH GRADE	SIXTH GRADE BEGINNING	SIXTH GRADE MIDDLE	SEVENTH GRADE BEGINNING	SEVENTH GRADE MIDDLE	EIGHTH GRADE BEGINNING	EIGHTH GRADE MIDDLE	NINTH GRADE BEGINNING	NINTH GRADE MIDDLE	BEGINNING OF TENTH GRADE
Total Number of Students per Mathematics Level	56	114	105	50	85	24	34	16	11	1	4
Number of Groups	2	4	4	2	3	1	3		1		
Number of Students per Group	28	≤ 29	≤ 27	25	≤ 29	24	≤ 17		16		

Table 4.5: Sample Class Groupings for All Middle School Students in Science

	FOURTH GRADE	FIFTH GRADE	SIXTH GRADE BEGINNING	SIXTH GRADE MIDDLE	SEVENTH GRADE BEGINNING	SEVENTH GRADE MIDDLE	EIGHTH GRADE BEGINNING	EIGHTH GRADE MIDDLE	NINTH GRADE BEGINNING	NINTH GRADE MIDDLE	TENTH GRADE BEGINNING	TENTH GRADE MIDDLE
Total Number of Students per Science Level	56	116	82	62	76	32	40	11	16	3	4	2
Number of Groups	2	5	6		4		2		1			
Number of Students per Group	28	≤ 24	24		27		≤ 26		25			

These sample groupings assume that all teachers and locations (in this case, twenty) will be available for each content area; if this is the case, the exact same process described for the anchor content area occurs for the new class period. If the number of available locations and teachers is less than twenty, then the process must undergo a modification. We know that realistically, the school will not have twenty available educators for every class period because of the variables that a school has to accommodate: prep periods, lunch, certifications, and so on. Thus, this middle school's scheduling team need to ask another important question: "How many educators are available to teach mathematics during third period?" Perhaps there are only fifteen educators available during third period due to the addition of third-period-specific variables such as electives, lunch schedules, prep periods, and so on. The team would adjust the chart of subcategories and class sizes (table 4.4) accordingly.

Table 4.6: Sample Class Groupings for All Middle School Students in Social Studies

| | FOURTH GRADE | FIFTH GRADE | SIXTH GRADE | | SEVENTH GRADE | | EIGHTH GRADE | | BEGINNING OF NINTH GRADE | BEGINNING OF TENTH GRADE |
			BEGINNING	MIDDLE	BEGINNING	MIDDLE	BEGINNING	MIDDLE		
Total Number of Students per Social Studies Level	26	116	58	87	72	71	41	19	9	1
Number of Groups	1	4	2	3	3	3	2	1	1	
Number of Students per Group	26	29	29	29	24	≤ 24	≤ 21	19	10	

With all the groupings drafted, setting the schedule becomes a process of moving groups of classes around to accommodate the variables within each class period. The different content areas within each class period and the range of content within the classes will most likely change throughout this process based on the school's student data. To accommodate the variables and available locations for each class period, the schedulers will likely need to deviate from the ideal horizontal schedule at some point. The best possible arrangement might involve scheduling the same content area in multiple class periods as in the general horizontal schedule example given at the beginning of the chapter (figure 4.1, page 69) or assigning the same teacher to teach the same content area within different periods (that is, more than once per day; see figure 4.2).

Class Periods	TEACHER A	TEACHER B	TEACHER C	TEACHER D
Period 1	Homeroom	Homeroom	Homeroom	Homeroom
Period 2	High-priority content area	High-priority content area	High-priority content area	High-priority content area
Period 3	Second priority content area	Lunch	Recess, phys ed, or elective	Second priority content area
Period 4	Lunch	Recess, phys ed, or elective	Recess, phys ed, or elective	Lunch
Period 5	Second priority content area	Recess, phys ed, or elective	Lunch	Second priority content area
Period 6	Other content area instruction	Other content area instruction	Other content area instruction	Other content area instruction

Figure 4.2: Teachers teaching the same content area within different periods.

When a schedule is not perfectly horizontal, conflicts can occur within individual students' schedules. For example, imagine a mathematics class that covers fifth-grade standards and a science class that addresses seventh-grade standards are scheduled during sixth period. One or more students need to learn both those ranges of content, but that period is the only time in the schedule when those particular sets of standards are addressed. The scheduling team will have to move one of the classes to a different period or assign some students to classes that do not perfectly match their learning needs, expanding the range of content those classes must cover. In our example, mathematics is a higher priority (second only to ELA), so it is more appropriate to move the science class to another period or create multilevel science classes to compensate for the conflict. A science class that was originally designed to cover one grade level of content may now cover two grade levels to accommodate this problem. The best option will depend on the specific student data and variables for the class periods. While it is not ideal to expand the range of content covered in a class, keep in mind that every classroom in a traditional system contains a huge range of learning needs for the teacher to address. The ranges that happen within PCBE schedules are still generally much smaller than in the traditional system, leading to better learning environments for both students and educators.

Once an initial schedule based on academic data exists, schedulers can consider age and behavioral factors. Again, these considerations slightly modify the schedule to correct major errors or factors that will disrupt instruction. Do not completely rearrange the schedule based on age or behaviors. The most important rules to stick to during this process are as follows.

- Do not make adjustments to the anchor content area.
- Try to make as few adjustments as possible to the second content area that you added.
- Try to create the best learning environment for each student.

A realistic approach to creating a horizontal schedule for an entire school requires accepting that you may only be able to schedule two class periods in a perfectly horizontal manner. After those two classes are set, the variables often become overpowering, and the schedule begins to look more traditional. The same issues found within the traditional schedule become more apparent. Classes with wider ranges of content appear in successive content areas, leading to teachers having to differentiate instruction to multiple groups. Therefore, as part of the thought process, it is helpful to look at the remaining content areas and the scope and sequence of standards across all the identified grade levels to determine which ones are the most conducive to flexible classroom grouping or connecting the curriculum. For example, there may be more flexibility and overlap within science topics than within social studies or vice versa.

Summary

Horizontal scheduling is the best way to create a PCBE schedule when looking strictly at student data. In a horizontal schedule, all the students study the same content area during the same period in the day, and each class focuses on a limited range of content. This approach benefits both the students (by addressing their learning needs) and the teachers (by limiting the range of needs within each class that they teach). The challenge with horizontal scheduling is that it requires a large number of certified teachers per content area, so it is restricted to school structures that allow for broad certification.

Realistic application of a horizontal schedule will likely accommodate horizontal scheduling for one or two core content areas and then adapt to a more traditional approach to scheduling for the remaining areas. The result is a combination of ideal student-focused scheduling and practical integration of real-life variables such as certification, prep periods, and lunch schedules. The end goal for this process is to design a schedule around the students' needs that creates the best learning environment possible. The next chapter provides an in-depth look at a vertical approach to scheduling.

Chapter 5

Creation of a Vertical PCBE Schedule

You're not pushed or rushed to just get everything done. It used to be you had a deadline and you had to be done at that time. With [PCBE] we take our time and really deeply learn it.

—Eighth-grade student

A vertical schedule distributes classes for a particular area of learning throughout all the periods in a school day, rather than trying to organize all the classes for that content area within one period of the day as horizontal scheduling does. The vertical-scheduling process really comes down to a few main components.

- Determining the number of available classes for a certain area of learning
- Clarifying how many classes are needed for that content area in relation to the grade-level data
- Assigning the appropriately certified teachers to all the identified classes while also assigning the classes to particular periods in the schedule
- Assigning all the students to the classes that have been placed throughout the schedule

In the example schedule in figure 5.1 (page 84), each content area is prioritized according to student data. This prioritization creates a scheduling process that allows for the highest priority content area to have the narrowest range of academic needs. With each successive content area assigned to the schedule, the probability of student scheduling conflicts increases. By the time the fourth and fifth prioritized content areas are placed in the schedule, there could be a much wider range of academic needs in each class.

In comparison to horizontal scheduling, vertical scheduling is a much more practical approach for high schools, middle schools that have specific content certifications, and elementary schools that have departmentalized their content areas. Those situations each have a fixed number of teachers who are available to teach the content areas throughout the day, and these human-resource limitations greatly

	GROUP 1	GROUP 2	GROUP 3	GROUP 4
Period 1	Math (first priority content area)	ELA (second priority content area)	Science (third priority content area)	Social studies (fourth priority content area)
Period 2	ELA (second priority content area)	Math (first priority content area)	ELA (second priority content area)	Science (third priority content area)
Period 3	Science (third priority content area)	Lunch	Elective (fifth priority content area)	Math (first priority content area)
Period 4	Lunch	Elective (fifth priority content area)	Social studies (fourth priority content area)	Lunch
Period 5	Elective (fifth priority content area)	Social studies (fourth priority content area)	Lunch	Elective (fifth priority content area)
Period 6	Social studies (fourth priority content area)	Science (third priority content area)	Math (first priority content area)	ELA (second priority content area)

Figure 5.1: General example of a vertical schedule.

affect how a PCBE schedule can be created. Vertical scheduling works with those limited numbers much better than horizontal scheduling does.

A key to vertical scheduling is to determine an anchor content area that receives priority—schedulers assign this content area to class periods throughout the day and avoid altering those classes' location or range of levels when adding all the other content areas to the schedule. Just as with horizontal scheduling, the first few content areas scheduled will more closely align with students' needs than the later areas due to the addition of variables throughout the schedule. The variables that affect vertical scheduling are the same variables that affect horizontal scheduling: teacher certifications, prep periods, lunch schedules, specials or electives, special education requirements, and so on. Within vertical scheduling, the variables are addressed in a slightly different way, but they all still factor into the scheduling equation. For example, teacher prep periods are taken into consideration immediately when creating a vertical schedule because the course of the entire day is being addressed, whereas in horizontal scheduling, schedulers address prep periods after they have added the first and second content areas to the schedule.

Another similarity between horizontal scheduling and vertical scheduling is the reliance on and analysis of student data. Grade-level data and specific standards data are still the driving force in determining the placement of students within the schedule. The number of available teachers and locations for instruction determines the number of groups that the student population will be divided into for each content area. Subcategories within the grade-level data are divided up according to the desired teacher-student ratio and used as a guide to determine the number of students per class. This ratio is a guideline to follow rather than a hard-and-fast cap on class size. The master list of students' names leads the scheduling team to analyze specific standards data to identify similar learning patterns and group students within each class.

With vertical scheduling, the team faces the big issue of trying to keep all other content areas from disrupting the anchor content area. This problem occurs when a student should be placed in two particular classes that are scheduled at the same time. A student cannot be in two places at once, so either the schedule or the classes' range of content must change. Preventing this problem entirely is difficult in vertical scheduling; there is a high chance that some students will need to take classes on two different content areas at two different levels that are scheduled during the same period. That high probability is the exact reason why horizontal scheduling exists—to avoid these types of conflicts, at least in part.

With that being said, though horizontal scheduling does a great job isolating a student's needs in a schedule, it does not deal with real-life factors as well as vertical scheduling does. Vertical scheduling does a good job creating appropriate learning environments while also incorporating unavoidable variables into the scheduling equation. Depending on how many periods are in the schedule, educators might address the learning needs of the students with scheduling conflicts during an elective or study hall period; if the school is still transitioning to PCBE, such a solution might also allow for more intensive one-on-one or small-group instruction to help the students close their specific gaps.

There are five main steps to vertical scheduling.

1. Establishing the foundation for scheduling
2. Organizing students within the anchor content area
3. Assigning classes to periods and teachers to classes
4. Assigning students to class periods
5. Adding more content areas

The following sections detail each step.

Establishing the Foundation for Scheduling

As with horizontal scheduling, schedulers need to establish certain foundational information to begin crafting a vertical schedule. The foundational questions for vertical scheduling are as follows.

- Which content area should be the anchor for the schedule?
- How many classes can be formed in the selected anchor content area?

Notice that these questions focus on the anchor content area and the available classes but not the class period. In this approach to scheduling, each content area will be scheduled in various class periods throughout the day. Because of that, the number of available teachers per class period becomes the biggest driving factor in this process because it determines the number of classes that the school can create.

Which Content Area Should Be the Anchor for the Schedule?

Just as with horizontal scheduling, schools should use academic data to determine which content area will be the anchor for the vertical schedule. The scheduling team should analyze state test scores, district test scores, and individual standards-based student data to determine the anchor content area. The criteria used to prioritize the content areas are up to each school or district, but student data must drive the conversation and the decision. Often the prioritization focuses on the content area that has the lowest student achievement, but other factors may come into play, especially when there isn't a single marked area of need. In this case, the team may look at the impact of different content areas on each other to determine a priority. For example, reading and writing are foundational to all areas of the curriculum, so the team might choose ELA as the top priority because its impact is comprehensive.

During the process of determining the anchor content area, schools would benefit by creating a prioritized list of all the content areas based on the schools' needs. The purpose of this list is to determine the order in which the schedulers will place the content areas into the vertical schedule. This list generally aligns with the subject areas that are on standardized tests. It normally starts with English language arts and mathematics at the top of the list, followed by science and social studies and then other academic courses and electives. It is unfortunate that content areas are thought of in this way, as all learning is important, but schools and districts must have some way of making decisions when scheduling conflicts arise, and they must acknowledge the reality of standardized testing.

For our example middle school, assume that the schedulers have analyzed the data and decided that mathematics will be the anchor content area for the vertical schedule.

How Many Classes Can Be Formed in the Anchor Content Area?

As in horizontal scheduling, the number of classes available dictates the classes' size and range of content. Two factors play into the decision of how many classes can form for the anchor content area.

1. The number of class periods in a school day
2. The number of teachers available to teach the content area

The number of class periods remains constant because the bell schedule is already set. As mentioned in chapter 3 (page 51), block schedules and period schedules each have their pros and cons. A period schedule allows for all content areas to be taught within one day. Block schedules may alternate classes throughout the week, which adds a new variable to the equation. Our example middle school uses a six-period daily schedule.

The second factor—the number of teachers who are certified and available—will vary for each content area. Schools that would likely opt for vertical scheduling (that is, high schools and similarly structured middle schools) are also likely to employ staff with narrower certifications. In chapter 4 (page 67), the teachers in our example middle school were generalists and certified for kindergarten through eighth grade. In this chapter, we will assume that the teachers have narrower, subject-specific certifications.

It would be ideal, from the students' perspective, if all the educators taught during all six periods throughout the day. This would give students a larger number of available locations for learning, which, in turn, would mean fewer students and a smaller range in learning needs in each class. From the teachers' perspective, however, that scenario is *not* ideal or even possible because they need time to prepare for all the classes throughout the day—and they have to eat lunch too! For that reason, the scheduling team must add a prep period for each teacher early in the vertical-scheduling process. Instead of having six available class periods per day, teachers really have five, because one period is set aside for preparation. In our example middle school, lunch is placed between third and fourth periods to simplify the examples. In a real-world situation, there might be a mixture of third period, lunch, and fourth period, to better accommodate the lunch schedule.

In this case, the example middle school still has twenty total teachers, but only five are certified to teach mathematics, the selected anchor content area. The school still has a total population of five hundred students. With the number of available class periods set at five per teacher, the total number of available classes for instructing mathematics each day is twenty-five. The school uses its overall student-to-teacher ratio of twenty-five to one to set the target class size (that is, the schedulers will try to keep the number of students per class around twenty-five). The scheduling team uses these numbers to organize the five hundred students within mathematics.

Organizing Students Within the Anchor Content Area

The next step in the vertical-scheduling process is to organize students based on their learning needs in the anchor content area and then to place the students within an environment that will best support that learning. First, schedulers should examine the mathematics grade-level data for the entire school. The grade-level data in table 5.1 (page 88) show that the middle school students' learning needs fall into eleven subcategories ranging from fourth-grade content all the way to beginning-of-tenth-grade content. The number of students within each subcategory will determine how many classes the school needs for that content level.

Table 5.1: Current Grade-Level Data for All Middle School Students in Mathematics

FOURTH GRADE	FIFTH GRADE	BEGINNING OF SIXTH GRADE	MIDDLE OF SIXTH GRADE	BEGINNING OF SEVENTH GRADE	MIDDLE OF SEVENTH GRADE	BEGINNING OF EIGHTH GRADE	MIDDLE OF EIGHTH GRADE	BEGINNING OF NINTH GRADE	MIDDLE OF NINTH GRADE	BEGINNING OF TENTH GRADE
56	114	105	50	85	24	34	16	11	1	4

As with all student data, the distribution is unique for each particular school and can vary greatly, which makes creating a PCBE schedule more difficult than creating a traditional schedule. The same processes and variables are used every time a PCBE schedule is established, but the outcomes depend on what the student data require at that time.

Similar to the process for horizontal scheduling, vertical scheduling determines the number of classes for each content level based on the number of available teachers. As mentioned previously, our example middle school has twenty-five classes available for mathematics, with a student population of five hundred, and a desired class size of twenty-five. Thus, the scheduling team divides the number of students in each subcategory by twenty-five to determine the number of classes that are needed per subcategory.

Table 5.2 shows how the grade-level data for each subcategory can be broken up into twenty-five classes. Where the number of students in each subcategory allows, classes should cover only one grade level and avoid combining students from different subcategories to make a class. In some cases, there will not be enough students in a subcategory to meet the general target ratio of twenty-five to one. In those cases, schedulers need to combine consecutive subcategories to create a class with a roster as close to the preferred class size as possible. In an ideal situation, student data would allow for an equal distribution of class sizes that span similar ranges of content, but we know that this is not often the case. This first example with twenty-five available classes (table 5.2) is the most ideal situation for distributing students and achieving the desired class size, but it is also less common than the second and third examples (tables 5.3 and 5.4, page 90) with fewer available educators.

Looking at the grade-level data and the subcategory of beginning of seventh grade, we see eighty-five students need to learn that range of mathematics content. Based on the target ratio of twenty-five to one, the scheduling team would create four classes for that content level, each of which would have no more than twenty-two students, which is below the target ratio. The groups for beginning of ninth grade, middle of ninth grade, and beginning of tenth grade do not have enough students to form separate classes, and therefore would create an equity issue of very small class sizes, as well as there not being enough available teachers to teach those individual content ranges. Considering the available resources, the school cannot justify having a class of just eleven students covering beginning-of-ninth-grade content. While that might be an ideal situation for those students' learning needs, it is not practical and would negatively impact other students, who would experience larger class sizes as a result.

Table 5.2: Sample Class Groupings Based on Twenty-Five Available Mathematics Classes

	FOURTH GRADE	FIFTH GRADE	SIXTH GRADE		SEVENTH GRADE		EIGHTH GRADE		NINTH GRADE		BEGINNING OF TENTH GRADE
			BEGINNING	MIDDLE	BEGINNING	MIDDLE	BEGINNING	MIDDLE	BEGINNING	MIDDLE	
Total Number of Students per Mathematics Level	56	114	105	50	85	24	34	16	11	1	4
Number of Groups	3	6	5	2	4	1	2	1	1		
Number of Students per Group	≤ 19	19	21	25	≤ 22	24	17	16	16		

Notice that this vertical-scheduling example has more classes available for one content area than the horizontal-scheduling example does. Having twenty-five classes devoted to mathematics—because they are not all in one period and teachers can instruct multiple sections—helps more evenly spread students throughout a content area. The bottom row of table 5.2 shows the maximum number of students in any one class is twenty-five, and the smallest classes have sixteen students, which keeps all at or below the target ratio. These numbers are lower than the horizontal-scheduling class sizes for mathematics (table 4.4, page 78), which were mostly in the mid- to upper twenties. Smaller class sizes even with a limited number of teachers certified in a given content area is another advantage to vertical scheduling.

If there is a concern that sixteen students in one class and twenty-five students in another is too large a difference, then schedulers would need to regroup the students across the subcategories. For the example in table 5.2, this would likely involve eliminating the middle-of-eighth-grade class, assigning some students to the higher-level class and some to the beginning-of-eighth-grade class, and making the resulting extra class available to the middle-of-sixth-grade subcategory. Anytime subcategories are grouped together, it instantly means that there will be a wide range of needs among the students within the class. The class size and the range of needs are always in tension in these situations—a benefit to one is a detriment to the other. Keep in mind the overall goal of creating the best possible learning environment for students when compromising on these concerns.

Different schools will have different numbers of available certified educators for each content area, so tables 5.3 and 5.4 (page 90) show groupings for vertical scheduling with the variable of available classes changed to twenty and seventeen, respectively. These examples show how altering this one variable can greatly affect class distributions. Notice that the range of class sizes is the biggest change; with twenty available classes, the range of class sizes is from twenty-two to thirty-four, with several classes above the desired twenty-five. Though the average class size is twenty-five students per class, this hides the fact that there could be large variations from class to class. With seventeen available classes, the number of classes above the target ratio increases significantly and the average rises to nearly thirty. As the number of available classes decreases, the range of needs covered in some classes also increases.

Table 5.3: Sample Class Groupings Based on Twenty Available Mathematics Classes

	FOURTH GRADE	FIFTH GRADE	SIXTH GRADE		SEVENTH GRADE		EIGHTH GRADE		NINTH GRADE		BEGINNING OF TENTH GRADE
			BEGINNING	MIDDLE	BEGINNING	MIDDLE	BEGINNING	MIDDLE	BEGINNING	MIDDLE	
Total Number of Students per Mathematics Level	56	114	105	50	85	24	34	16	11	1	4
Number of Groups	2	5	4	2	4	1	1	1			
Number of Students per Group	28	≤ 23	≤ 27	25	≤ 22	24	34	32			

Table 5.4: Sample Class Groupings Based on Seventeen Available Mathematics Classes

	FOURTH GRADE	FIFTH GRADE	SIXTH GRADE		SEVENTH GRADE		EIGHTH GRADE		NINTH GRADE		BEGINNING OF TENTH GRADE
			BEGINNING	MIDDLE	BEGINNING	MIDDLE	BEGINNING	MIDDLE	BEGINNING	MIDDLE	
Total Number of Students per Mathematics Level	56	114	105	50	85	24	34	16	11	1	4
Number of Groups	2	4	3	2	3	1	1	1			
Number of Students per Group	28	≤ 29	35	25	≤ 29	24	34	32			

No matter how the subcategories are organized, the teachers for each class do not just cover that content range from beginning to end or follow a curriculum pacing guide. Each class focuses on addressing the standards that students need to learn and then moves on to the next levels at an appropriate pace. The narrowed range of content indicated by student needs allows teachers to zero in on specific standards for each individual student and dictates the plan for instruction.

Assigning Classes to Periods and Teachers to Classes

Going back to the first example in table 5.2 (page 89), the next step is placing the twenty-five available classes for mathematics within the actual schedule. The five teachers certified to teach mathematics will each instruct five classes per day and have one prep period. When assigning the various content-level classes to teachers, the scheduling team should consider assigning classes of the same or similar levels to a teacher. In other words, the teacher ends up teaching the same content or closely related content multiple times throughout the day. This teacher can then prep for those standards and repeat or slightly modify his or her lessons and units based on students' needs in each class. This reduces the amount of prep work and time needed per class and increases the teacher's ability to focus in on the students' individual needs.

One option for vertically scheduling mathematics in our example middle school appears in figure 5.2 (page 92). Notice that Teacher A has a range of fourth- and fifth-grade content whereas Teacher E covers the middle of seventh grade through tenth grade. It happens to work out that Teacher D has all the beginning-of-seventh-grade classes (as well as one middle-of-sixth-grade section). That doesn't necessarily mean that Teacher D is going to address the exact same standards in each of those classes. The individual needs of the students in each class will drive what standards that teacher addresses.

Figure 5.2 includes a power hour. Marzano and colleagues (2017) define *power hour* as a flexible period devoted to "focused instructional time" (p. 140), in which students concentrate on filling in gaps in their learning or extending their learning while having access to multiple content-area teachers. Schools that are implementing some components of PCBE but are still using a traditional age-based schedule commonly use this power hour approach to alleviate learning gaps (perhaps as an alternative to a traditional study hall period). Power hour is not necessary in a vertical PCBE schedule, but it is never a bad idea to incorporate more opportunities for students to focus on their personal learning needs and interests. If your school does not use this structure, you can replace this section of the schedule with a standard lunch.

In figure 5.2, all the mathematics teachers have common prep time during fourth period. A school's prep-period schedule depends on how the teachers are organized for collaboration. Options include having a common prep period for teachers in the same grade level; having a common prep period for teachers in the same or similar content areas; and giving teachers random prep periods, which means teachers may or may not prep at the same time as similar teachers. Figure 5.3 (page 92) shows a variation on the preceding schedule, in which grade-level teachers have the same prep period. Each mathematics teacher has a different prep period according to the grade level he or she primarily teaches.

PERIODS	MATHEMATICS TEACHERS				
	Teacher A	Teacher B	Teacher C	Teacher D	Teacher E
Period 1	Fourth Grade	Fifth Grade	Beginning of Sixth Grade	Beginning of Seventh Grade	Ninth and Tenth Grade
Period 2	Fifth Grade	Fifth Grade	Beginning of Sixth Grade	Beginning of Seventh Grade	Beginning of Eighth Grade
Period 3	Fourth Grade	Fifth Grade	Middle of Sixth Grade	Middle of Sixth Grade	Beginning of Eighth Grade
Lunch and Power Hour					
Period 4	Prep	Prep	Prep	Prep	Prep
Period 5	Fifth Grade	Beginning of Sixth Grade	Middle of Sixth Grade	Beginning of Seventh Grade	Middle of Eighth Grade
Period 6	Fourth Grade	Fifth Grade	Beginning of Sixth Grade	Beginning of Seventh Grade	Middle of Seventh Grade

Figure 5.2: Sample vertical schedule for mathematics with a common teacher prep period.

PERIODS	MATHEMATICS TEACHERS				
	Teacher A	Teacher B	Teacher C	Teacher D	Teacher E
Period 1	Fourth Grade	Fifth Grade	Beginning of Sixth Grade	Beginning of Seventh Grade	Prep
Period 2	Fifth Grade	Prep	Beginning of Sixth Grade	Beginning of Seventh Grade	Ninth and Tenth Grade
Period 3	Fourth Grade	Fifth Grade	Prep	Middle of Sixth Grade	Beginning of Eighth Grade
Lunch and Power Hour					
Period 4	Prep	Fifth Grade	Middle of Sixth Grade	Beginning of Seventh Grade	Beginning of Eighth Grade
Period 5	Fifth Grade	Beginning of Sixth Grade	Middle of Sixth Grade	Prep	Middle of Eighth Grade
Period 6	Fourth Grade	Fifth Grade	Beginning of Sixth Grade	Beginning of Seventh Grade	Middle of Seventh Grade

Figure 5.3: Sample vertical schedule for mathematics with grade-level teacher prep periods.

Organizing prep periods by grade level means that the anchor content area dictates the prep-period schedule for all content areas. The anchor content area is the first to be placed in the schedule, with all the other content areas following suit. Each new content area that is added must align each teacher's prep period with the grade-level prep periods established by the anchor content area.

Assigning Students to Class Periods

Now that the school has set the classes for the anchor content area in the schedule and assigned the teachers to all the classes, it is time to assign students to those classes. While data on students' learning needs have driven the vertical-scheduling process from the beginning, actually placing specific students in specific classes is the final step in scheduling the anchor content area due to all the variables that need to be clarified.

Assigning students to classes in a vertical schedule is the exact same process as in horizontal scheduling (see page 74). Based on the previous steps of the scheduling process, the scheduling team knows the number of classes per subcategory and the approximate number of students per class at each level (see table 5.2, page 89). To place specific students in each class, schedulers reference the grade-level data's master list of student names, which shows which students are in which subcategories. For content levels that have multiple classes, the team examines students' specific standards data to group students with similar learning needs. For example, in table 5.2 (page 89), the beginning-of-eighth-grade subcategory consists of thirty-four students who need to be placed into two classes, each of approximately seventeen students. Schedulers will refer to all thirty-four students' specific standards data but can also use criteria such as age and behavioral factors to determine how they will divide up the students into the two classes.

Creating a schedule for the anchor content area (in this case, mathematics) is relatively easy because schedulers do not have to consider other content areas in figuring out which period is the best location for each mathematics class. Once the scheduling team places all the students into the scheduled mathematics classes, it is time to start adding the next content areas to the schedule.

Adding More Content Areas

The addition of each subsequent content area to the vertical schedule follows the same basic process as for the anchor content area, but assigning students to classes becomes increasingly complex as you must ensure that you don't assign any students to classes that conflict with each other (that is, classes that occur at the same time). To select the second content area to schedule, return to the prioritized list. For our example, the middle school schedulers will next add ELA to the schedule, followed by science and social studies. Next, determine how many certified teachers and classes are available in that subject area. The example middle school has five teachers qualified to teach ELA throughout all the grade levels.

As in mathematics, these five certified teachers can each take on five classes, for a total of twenty-five ELA classes during the school day. Now, it is time to look at the grade-level subcategory data to determine the number of classes that will be needed for each group. Table 5.5 shows the grade-level data for ELA and how schedulers can distribute the twenty-five classes throughout the eleven subcategories while keeping class sizes at or below the target ratio.

Table 5.5: Sample Class Groupings Based on Twenty-Five Available ELA Classes

	FOURTH GRADE	FIFTH GRADE	SIXTH GRADE		SEVENTH GRADE		EIGHTH GRADE		NINTH GRADE		BEGINNING OF TENTH GRADE
			BEGINNING	MIDDLE	BEGINNING	MIDDLE	BEGINNING	MIDDLE	BEGINNING	MIDDLE	
Total Number of Students per ELA Level	30	111	83	63	87	50	50	12	9	2	3
Number of Groups	2	5	4	3	4	3	2	1	1		
Number of Students per Group	15	≤ 23	≤ 21	21	≤ 22	≤ 17	25	12	14		

With the grade-level data broken up into classes, the next step is to assign all the classes to certain periods within the schedule and assign the teachers to the range of content for certain classes. The same variables that affected the schedule for mathematics, such as content-area or grade-level teacher prep periods, must be considered when scheduling ELA. Figure 5.4 shows an example ELA schedule in which all the ELA teachers have a common prep period. To ensure there are enough classes available at any given time, the schedulers take into account when the common mathematics prep period takes place in the school schedule (period 4, per figure 5.2, page 92) and place the common ELA prep time in a different period. Figure 5.5 shows an example ELA schedule that assumes a common prep time for the same grade levels. This schedule aligns with the grade-level prep periods set for mathematics in figure 5.3 (page 92).

The final step in establishing the second content area is to assign students to content-area classes within the schedule. With the second and subsequent content areas, the scheduling team must analyze previously placed class rosters to make sure that there are no conflicts in any periods. That is, they must ensure they don't assign students to two classes during the same period. For example, when placing students in the third-period ELA class that covers the middle of sixth grade (figure 5.4), schedulers need to check these placements against all the third-period mathematics class rosters to make sure that no students also need a mathematics class that period.

PERIODS	ELA TEACHERS				
	Teacher F	Teacher G	Teacher H	Teacher I	Teacher J
Period 1	Fifth Grade	Beginning of Sixth Grade	Middle of Sixth Grade	Beginning of Seventh Grade	Beginning of Eighth Grade
Period 2	Prep	Prep	Prep	Prep	Prep
Period 3	Fourth Grade	Beginning of Sixth Grade	Middle of Sixth Grade	Beginning of Seventh Grade	Middle of Eighth Grade
Lunch and Power Hour					
Period 4	Fifth Grade	Beginning of Sixth Grade	Beginning of Seventh Grade	Middle of Seventh Grade	Ninth and Tenth Grade
Period 5	Fifth Grade	Fifth Grade	Middle of Sixth Grade	Beginning of Eighth Grade	Middle of Seventh Grade
Period 6	Fourth Grade	Fifth Grade	Beginning of Sixth Grade	Beginning of Seventh Grade	Middle of Seventh Grade

Figure 5.4: Sample vertical schedule for ELA with a common teacher prep period.

PERIODS	ELA TEACHERS				
	Teacher F	Teacher G	Teacher H	Teacher I	Teacher J
Period 1	Fifth Grade	Beginning of Sixth Grade	Middle of Sixth Grade	Beginning of Seventh Grade	Prep
Period 2	Fifth Grade	Prep	Middle of Sixth Grade	Beginning of Eighth Grade	Beginning of Eighth Grade
Period 3	Fourth Grade	Beginning of Sixth Grade	Prep	Beginning of Seventh Grade	Middle of Eighth Grade
Lunch and Power Hour					
Period 4	Prep	Beginning of Sixth Grade	Beginning of Seventh Grade	Middle of Seventh Grade	Ninth and Tenth Grade
Period 5	Fifth Grade	Fifth Grade	Middle of Sixth Grade	Prep	Middle of Seventh Grade
Period 6	Fourth Grade	Fifth Grade	Beginning of Sixth Grade	Beginning of Seventh Grade	Middle of Seventh Grade

Figure 5.5: Sample vertical schedule for ELA with grade-level teacher prep periods.

With only one content area to contend with, the schedule for the second content area will hopefully contain few conflicts. As with horizontal scheduling, addressing conflicts during vertical scheduling involves moving classes around to locate the best fit within the schedule. If there is a conflict that the middle school's scheduling team cannot resolve by moving an ELA class to a different period in the schedule, then unfortunately, the school will have to modify an ELA class already scheduled in a different period so it includes a wider range of content. For example, placing a student who needs to learn the beginning of sixth grade in a class that is covering the middle of sixth grade is not too extreme a range. It is not ideal, but it is still feasible. On the other hand, adding a student whose learning is at the beginning of sixth grade to the middle-of-eighth-grade class would be inappropriate because the classroom teacher would need to cover an extreme range of content within the class in order to address this student's needs. The goal is to find the closest class in terms of content so that the range for the newly modified class is as reasonable as possible. Remember that mathematics is the example middle school's anchor content area, so the school needs to make every effort to keep those classes intact.

With the addition of a third and fourth content area, the potential for more issues will rise. Schedule modifications will potentially become more extreme, meaning that they might create wider ranges in content areas. In the example middle school, science and social studies go through the same process and are added to the master schedule with varying ranges of student needs based on the grade-level and specific-standards data. This type of juggling is inevitable in PCBE.

Besides dealing with conflicts between academic classes, schedulers need to take into account variables such as lunch schedules, specials or electives, and special education requirements and modify them accordingly. For example, schedulers might have to establish the lunch schedule and then modify the student placement based on that information. They add electives to the schedule in a similar fashion as the other content areas, by identifying the number of classes needed and teachers available, then analyzing student data to determine student placement into classes.

Once the scheduling team has created an initial vertical schedule based on academic data, then they can take age and behavioral factors into consideration, keeping in mind that major scheduling changes based on these factors should occur only in extreme cases. In general, this secondary process is used to slightly modify the schedule to correct major errors or factors that will disrupt instruction. As in horizontal scheduling, the most important rules to stick to during this process are these: don't make adjustments to the anchor content area; try to make as few adjustments as possible to the second content area that you added; and try to create the best learning environment for each student.

The end result of this vertical-scheduling process is a master schedule in which the anchor content area's classes are most tightly aligned with students' learning needs, and classes for other content areas fit as well as possible in order of priority. Figure 5.6 shows an example of a complete student schedule that incorporates academic classes, a power hour and lunch combination, electives, and project-based learning time. In creating the student schedule, schedulers analyzed each class to determine if there were any conflicts.

Though there is no one perfect way to address all the needs of every individual student, this example seeks to illustrate that by targeting certain key content areas and reducing the range of need, schools ensure students are better supported in the classroom. Though schools may attempt to solve the complex problem of school scheduling in different ways, shifting their focus from filling classes with students regardless of their need to grouping students into classes according to need is key when moving toward a more PCBE approach.

PERIODS	STUDENT'S SCHEDULE
Period 1 (7:50–8:50 a.m.)	ELA (fifth grade with Teacher F)
Period 2 (8:55–9:55 a.m.)	Mathematics (beginning of sixth grade with Teacher C)
Period 3 (10:00–11:00 a.m.)	Social studies (beginning of sixth grade with Teacher P)
Lunch and Power Hour (11:00–11:55 a.m.) *Each student's schedule includes one of the following.* 1. First lunch (11:00–11:25 a.m.) and second power hour (11:25–11:55 a.m.) 2. First power hour (11:00–11:30 a.m.) and second lunch (11:30–11:55 a.m.)	First lunch Second power hour
Period 4 (11:55 a.m.–12:55 p.m.)	Art (with Teacher U) Mondays and Wednesdays Physical education (with Teacher V) Tuesdays and Thursdays Advisory or clubs (with Teacher Y) Fridays
Period 5 (1:00–2:00 p.m.)	Science (middle of sixth grade with Teacher K)
Period 6 (2:05–3:05 p.m.)	Project-based learning time

Figure 5.6: Sample vertical student schedule.

From an educator's perspective, a daily vertical schedule is similar to a traditional schedule. Teachers who are certified to teach mathematics, for instance, teach mathematics throughout the day with at least one prep period. Figure 5.7 shows an example of a mathematics teacher's schedule.

PERIODS	TEACHER E'S SCHEDULE
Period 1 (7:50–8:50 a.m.)	Prep period
Period 2 (8:55–9:55 a.m.)	Ninth- and tenth-grade mathematics
Period 3 (10:00–11:00 a.m.)	Beginning-of-eighth-grade mathematics
Lunch and Power Hour (11:00–11:55 a.m.) *Each teacher's schedule includes one of the following.* 1. First lunch (11:00–11:25 a.m.) and second power hour (11:25–11:55 a.m.) 2. First power hour (11:00–11:30 a.m.) and second lunch (11:30–11:55 a.m.)	Availability for first power hour Second lunch
Period 4 (11:55 a.m.–12:55 p.m.)	Beginning-of-eighth-grade mathematics
Period 5 (1:00–2:00 p.m.)	Middle-of-eighth-grade mathematics
Period 6 (2:05–3:05 p.m.)	Middle-of-seventh-grade mathematics

Figure 5.7: Sample vertical teacher schedule.

Note that this teacher has a combined ninth-and-tenth-grade mathematics class, which was formed based on student needs and the available classes. Though it is not ideal to have a wider range of content within a classroom, this arrangement is still closer to the needs of the students than a traditional class. This scheduling process is one part of an entire system that works to create an effective PCBE environment. As part of this system, educators will have strategies for developing student agency and addressing various needs within one classroom. Also, students will have experience working in this type of classroom, so the shift to a wider-ranging class is not a major hindrance for either the teacher or students. In comparison to the range of needs in an age-based classroom, a class covering only two levels sounds appealing. The teacher also has access to specific data on the needs of the students within those two levels, and therefore can design specific learning experiences for the students.

Summary

Vertical scheduling for PCBE requires that the scheduling team use student data to develop the schedule while also incorporating many real-life variables that schools have to deal with on a daily basis. This approach benefits schools that have a limited number of teachers certified to instruct specific content areas. With vertical scheduling, schools must pay special attention to not schedule students for two classes in the same period in the day. If conflicts do occur, schedulers may need to alter courses that are designed around one level of learning so that the courses allow for more flexibility of student placement within the schedule. The application of a vertical schedule has the potential to address many students' needs while also limiting the range of learning needs within each class. The end goal for vertical scheduling is to create the best learning environment possible while also accommodating as many variables as possible.

In the next and final chapter, we provide guidance for individual teachers who want to enact elements of flexible pacing and PCBE-style scheduling in their classrooms.

Chapter 6

PCBE Implementation Within Stand-Alone Classrooms

Our teacher gives us a lot of autonomy to do things. That means "to give you freedom," but we need to use it wisely.

—Fifth-grade student

When helping schools implement personalized competency-based systems, we frequently meet passionate teachers who strongly believe in PCBE. They often ask what they can do in their own classrooms, *right now*, to implement components of the framework. Our hearts are with these teachers. We were these teachers in 2004, in rural Alaska, talking into the wee hours of the night with like-minded colleagues and planning for how to better support our students.

Daryl Conner (2012), who coined the term *burning platform*—a sense of deep urgency that drives systemic change—reflected that the committed, successful leaders of large-scale organizational initiatives he studied did not simply want to try something new for its own sake. They wanted change because they felt "a sense of distress related to their current state" (Conner, 2012). This is the impetus that moves people not just to attempt a large-scale change, but to maintain the commitment and energy to see it through. Educators often acutely feel the distress associated with the traditional system. They see the inequity every day in their classrooms as they struggle to meet the myriad needs of their students. They can feel overburdened and often unsuccessful at their mammoth task. The impetus for wanting change always comes back to their students. Many teachers want a systemic change because they want *all* their students, not just a handful, to succeed, and they recognize that the current system does not support all students. If you are one of these teachers, this chapter is for you.

The goal of this chapter is to enable classroom teachers working within a traditional age-based system to implement PCBE-style methods for their own instruction; this way, their students experience some of the pacing and need-based support that a PCBE process offers. If schoolwide or districtwide PCBE implementation is not available, teachers will face certain limitations to how much their teaching plans can fit the PCBE mold, and they will have to work with age-based groups of students who are certain to have learning gaps. The mandated standards and assessments for the age-based schedule will still apply, and teachers will still need to work within those contexts; also, teachers will lack the data on student grade-level gaps that the comprehensive assessments of school- or districtwide PCBE implementation would provide. However, these educators still have options available to put even the traditional schedule's restrictions to work on behalf of a more PCBE-like learning process. The following sections describe many such options, which teachers can implement as a series of steps toward incorporating PCBE into age-based classrooms.

Acknowledging a Range of Classroom Implementation Levels

Individual educators have a range of PCBE implementation levels that they can attempt in the classroom. Think of these levels as a continuum ranging from the most traditional of schedules to the most flexible in terms of student need. Figure 6.1 shows this continuum.

Traditional Schedule			PCBE Schedule
Classrooms are age based, and the pace of content is predetermined by curriculum guides. Students transition to the next level based on an average grade of D or better on the adopted program or curriculum.	Classrooms are age based and have some combination of traditional education and PCBE in that they have a standards focus and offer some flexibility in the schedule for students working at their own pace on their needs. Students transition to the next level based on an average grade of D or better on the grade-level content.	Classrooms combine traditional education and PCBE with some flexibility in the schedule to group students and move them to specific classrooms according to their standards-based needs during focused instructional time. Students transition to the next level based on an average grade of D or better on the grade-level content.	Classrooms group students according to progress on standards. Students transition to the next level once they have achieved mastery of all the standards in that content-area level, regardless of when in the school year this happens.

Figure 6.1: Continuum of PCBE implementation.

Teachers may also be afforded different levels of autonomy within their traditional systems. Those who work within highly structured curriculum frameworks, such as scripted programs or pacing guides, are afforded lower levels of autonomy, while teachers in standards-referenced systems might have higher autonomy. Also of note are schools where teachers have a high level of autonomy with little to no accountability. While this is relatively rare, there are schools where classrooms operate as "islands" where administration rarely visits aside from perfunctory yearly evaluations, little to no collaboration happens, and teachers are left behind closed doors to their own devices. This is obviously not ideal, but teachers within a system like this could implement whatever aspects of PCBE, aside from physically shifting students to another classroom, that they wish. A continuum of autonomy might look like figure 6.2.

Low Autonomy ⟶ High Autonomy		
Teachers follow a prescribed schedule of classes and scripted programs in all content areas that include a pacing guide, which leaves small avenues for teacher autonomy. Teachers are monitored on adherence to district mandates and penalized if they stray from the prescribed formula.	Teachers have mixed levels of structure and autonomy within content areas dependent on programs or curriculum resources, with some areas having more opportunities for teacher discretion.	Standards drive the curriculum structure, but teachers have more autonomy in how and to whom they deliver instruction, pacing, assessment, and resources. Teachers group and regroup students within their classrooms throughout the learning process as students move at varied paces through the standards.

Figure 6.2: Continuum of teacher autonomy.

Depending on what system is in place within their school, some educators may have a more isolated experience delving into components of PCBE than others do, but even these teachers have the ability to serve as an exemplar for what a shift in practice and thinking looks like. Often, these teachers are modeling the change they wish was happening systemwide. Everything surrounding these educators has stayed exactly the same, but within their own classrooms, they are implementing parts of a new system for the students they serve. Obviously, the range of autonomy afforded can greatly affect the degree to which they are able to delve into PCBE-type scheduling, but there are areas where every teacher can apply some of the framework regardless of the level of choice available to them.

Some of the most tightly structured systems in place in schools involve prescribed curriculum, programs, and pacing. When teachers work in schools that have very tight curricula, they can still implement PCBE in areas outside the curriculum itself. These areas include cultural aspects of learning such as offering voice and choice and developing strong procedural elements with students co-creating protocols for how they want their classroom to operate. These areas are illustrated within chapter 2 of *A Handbook for Personalized Competency-Based Education*, titled "How Will the Learning Environment Support Student Agency?" (Marzano et al., 2017, p. 37).

Agency is something that any teacher can address at any time within the learning expectations or in the learning environment itself. Developing student agency is a perfect place to start when it comes to implementing PCBE, and it can be hugely motivating for students of any age. If there is a tight curricula in place, students may have less agency over their assessments or how instruction is delivered, but there are other opportunities for agency, such as the set-up of the physical learning environment, leadership opportunities in class jobs, mentorship, learning de-escalation strategies to assist with classroom or recess conflicts, personal goal setting and monitoring, presenting to a wider audience, student-led conferences with parents or caregivers, and tracking mastery of content as they move through the learning expectations. These are just a handful of ways educators can help build student agency in the classroom.

Working Within the Standards

For teachers seeking to implement PCBE within a traditional schedule, the key piece of information is what their students know in relation to the current grade-level standards to which the students are held. Determining this information in the absence of the comprehensive assessments leaves teachers one option: they must start with the standards themselves. This means teachers must first identify what sets of standards their students are held accountable for on the state and district assessments.

Various content areas are assessed more or less frequently at the state level, but there are state, provincial, or national standards for all content areas, including specialist areas such as visual and performing arts, physical education, technology, and media or library skills. Even if the standards in all content areas are not part of individual classroom teachers' purview, it's important that the teachers understand the full scope and sequence of expectations for students. This can also support and connect with the work that specialists or other content-area teachers are addressing in their classrooms. If the classroom teachers understand the learning expectations for visual arts, for example, they can easily speak to those concepts in other content areas they teach, create collaborative opportunities with other staff members, and build cross-content connections for their students. Many state or provincial visual and performing arts standards include making cross-content connections; figures 6.3 and 6.4 show examples from Maine and South Carolina, respectively.

E2: The Arts and Other Disciplines			
Performance Indicators and Descriptors			
PreK–2	3–5	6–8	9–Diploma
Students identify connections between and among the arts and other disciplines.	Students describe characteristics shared between and among the arts and other disciplines.	Students explain skills and concepts that are similar across disciplines.	Students analyze skills and concepts that are similar across disciplines.

Source: Maine Department of Education, n.d., p. 19.

Figure 6.3: Cross-content connections from Maine visual and performing arts standards.

Seeing how standards connect within and across content areas is beneficial to the classroom teacher for clarity, certainly, but just as importantly, awareness of these connections helps students build meaning and relevance. Knowing *why* they are learning something, its connection to other content, and the real-world application of that learning can be just as important to students' learning as the *what* and the *how* of the knowledge or skill. As mentioned in chapter 1 (page 12), this speaks to the "purpose" aspect of Pink's (2009) conception of motivation. Students don't always easily or intuitively make these

Indicator VA.C NL.7.1	Indicator VA.C NM.7.1	Indicator VA.C NH.7.1	Indicator VA.C IL.7.1	Indicator VA.C IM.7.1	Indicator VA.C IH.7.1	Indicator VA.C AL.7.1	Indicator VA.C AM.7.1	Indicator VA.C AH.7.1
I can show connections between visual art and other subjects in my school.	I can recognize and describe that visual art exists in all arts disciplines and other content areas.	I can identify ways visual art concepts and skills are used in other subjects in my school.	I can use art concepts and skills with other arts disciplines and content areas.	I can analyze and describe the relationship between visual art and specific content from another arts disciplines and content areas.	I can apply concepts from other arts disciplines and content areas to my artwork.	I can describe concepts from other arts disciplines and content areas through my artwork and justify my artistic choices.	I can describe how the demographics of a community can determine opportunities for arts-related careers.	I can analyze complex ideas from other arts disciplines and content areas to inspire my creative work and evaluate its impact on my artistic perspective.

Source: South Carolina Department of Education, 2017, p. 552.

Figure 6.4: Cross-content connections from South Carolina visual arts standards.

types of connections, so teachers should explicitly illustrate these relationships or open a dialogue that helps students inquire about and make connections on their own.

Within the scope and sequence of grade-level standards, schools may also create priority standards by emphasizing standards that represent more essential learning than others. Teachers often have too much content to cover, and not all standards are of equal importance. According to *A School Leader's Guide to Standards-Based Grading* (Heflebower et al., 2014), teachers must weigh five considerations when prioritizing standards.

1. **Endurance:** Will this content or skill be utilized in future learning expectations in terms of scaffolding other content and skills?

2. **Leverage:** Might this content or skill be impactful in a variety of ways and contexts?

3. **Readiness:** Does this content or skill prepare students for the next level of learning?

4. **Teacher judgment:** Do you as a teacher find this content or skill an important learning outcome based on what skills you see students needing?

5. **Assessment:** Will this content or skill be included within district and state assessments?

Depending on a teacher's level of autonomy, he or she may choose to emphasize some standards over others, consolidate similar standards, or remove standards that don't qualify for the suggested considerations. Though it is certainly not ideal to do this work alone (as opposed to school- or districtwide collaboration), educators with high autonomy but few avenues for team time or willing collaborators can certainly build on current available resources at the state, provincial, or national level to support their effort. The more a teacher moves toward tighter alignment between the expectations of the standards, instruction, and assessment, the more efficient preparation and instruction will be and the easier it will be to move students toward mastery with fewer gaps in skills and knowledge.

Coding Curriculum Resources

Once teachers have determined and prioritized their set of standards, the next step is to analyze and compare their curriculum resources against the standards. The purpose of this is to identify where the required curriculum will meet students' needs for acquiring grade-level knowledge and where teachers might need to expand the learning opportunities for students who have gaps. Many curricula that align with state or national standards will have an overview that highlights the standards the program addresses, which is helpful but often doesn't give teachers enough detail. Examining resources such as practice activities and assessments is important if teachers are to use those tools for determining student proficiency—especially when activities or assessments cover more than one standard, as is often the case. It is also important that teachers avoid assuming the curriculum resources align with their classroom needs.

To analyze instructional resources, teachers should have on hand the entire scope and sequence of grade-level content area standards. Resources, such as example programs, textbooks, or digital content, often have an explanation or guide that gives a summary of what they cover and how teachers can use it. These guides refer to different sections of the resource and are very helpful for pinpointing which standards are covered where. Teachers can use their standards lists and identify which part of the resource covers which standards and take notes directly on the standards list, creating a guide for resource use. As teachers work through the resource, they may notice that the resource does not cover some standards, or covers them inadequately, or goes into too much complexity on others. There may also be excess content not aligned with any grade-level expectations. This is often the case with textbooks, so teachers will find it helpful to code the textbook chapters and sections to which standards they cover.

Figure 6.5 (page 106) features a matrix for identifying where textbook chapters align with standards. In this example, a teacher analyzed a sixth-grade mathematics textbook and coded each sixth-grade Common Core standard for mathematics (NGA & CCSSO, 2010b) to the chapter and section that addressed it. For the standards listed down the far left column, each chapter section that addresses each standard is listed beneath the applicable chapters. So, the first ratio and proportions standards, 6.RP.A.1, is covered in section 1 of chapter 6. Notice that chapter 7 is not included because it covered none of the grade-level standards. Especially with outdated texts or those that predate the adoption of new or modified standards, often there are sections or even entire chapters that might not be applicable to the grade-level expectations. Since this classroom utilized online resources as well, the teacher added columns labeled *IXL*, an online learning platform, and *App*, short for application, which prompts students to access a digital game or tool. This analysis helped the teacher effectively utilize the textbook in his instruction. Students also used the matrix as a guide for where to find practice problems and support resources for standards they were currently working toward mastery on or reviewing during review cycles.

The work that teachers do behind the scenes analyzing standards and finding or creating aligned resources sets the stage for implementing both standards-based instruction and personalized learning that will allow students to navigate the scope and sequence of expectations in a more flexible way. An easy way to conceptualize this flexibility is with the four Ps: pace, pedagogy, practice, and product.

- **Pace:** The rate at which a student masters content
- **Pedagogy:** The way instruction is delivered
- **Practice:** How the student applies what they have learned in order to master content
- **Product:** The evidence the student generates to prove mastery of content

Coding curriculum resources establishes the foundation for a classroom that addresses all these elements.

STANDARD	CHAPTER 1	CHAPTER 2	CHAPTER 3	CHAPTER 5	CHAPTER 6	CHAPTER 8	CHAPTER 9	CHAPTER 10	CHAPTER 11	CHAPTER 12	IXL APP
6.RP.A.1					1						X
6.RP.A.2					2, 3						X
6.RP.A.3					4						X
6.NS.A.1				1, 2, 3, 4, 5, 6, 7							X
6.NS.B.2			1, 2, 3, 4, 5								X
6.NS.B.3		1, 2, 3, 4, 5, 6, 7, 8, 9									X
6.NS.B.4			1, 2, 3, 4, 5								X
6.NS.C.5						1, 2, 3, 4					X
6.NS.C.6						1, 2, 3, 11, 12					X
6.NS.C.7						3					X
6.NS.C.8											X
6.EE.A.1	1, 2, 3, 4, 5, 6, 7, 8, 9, 10, 11										X
6.EE.A.2	1, 2, 3, 4, 5, 6, 7, 8, 9, 10, 11										X
6.EE.A.3	1, 2, 3, 4, 5, 6, 7, 8, 9, 10, 11										X

Standard											X
6.EE.A.4	1, 2, 3, 4, 5, 6, 7, 8, 9, 10, 11										X
6.EE.B.5						12				1, 2	X
6.EE.B.6	1, 2, 3, 4, 5, 6, 7, 8, 9 10, 11										X
6.EE.B.7											X
6.EE.B.8										1, 2	X
6.EE.C.9											X
6.G.A.1								7, 8, 9, 10			X
6.G.A.2								16			X
6.G.A.3							6, 7, 8				X
6.G.A.4											X
6.SP.A.1									1, 2		X
6.SP.A.2									1, 2		X
6.SP.A.3									1, 2		X
6.SP.B.4									3, 4, 5, 6, 7, 8		X
6.SP.B.5											X

Source for standards: NGA & CCSSO, 2010b.

Figure 6.5: Matrix aligning standards with textbook chapters.

Ensuring Assessment Alignment and Adequate Evidence

Once a teacher has aligned curriculum resources with the standards, the teacher must ensure each standard is represented by a collection of evidence that would give him or her enough information to confidently score a student as proficient—the product part of the four Ps. This requires multiple assessment opportunities over time. Teachers may ask themselves the following questions to determine whether their assessments will allow them to establish adequate evidence of mastery.

- "How many assessment items are available for this standard?"

- "How and when will I utilize these assessment items?"

- "Do students have enough opportunity to show mastery of all the requirements of the standard?"

- "What other avenues (such as performance tasks, probing discussions, and observations) might students take to prove mastery, and what resources might I need to monitor student progress?"

As the teacher works through this assessment mapping, it may become apparent that there are abundant practice and assessment resources for certain standards and few for others. This analysis identifies where the teacher might need to create or find additional assessment resources for particular standards. This is particularly helpful for standards that take a long time to master due to their breadth or complexity, since students will need extensive practice and attempts at mastery. These longitudinal or recursive standards, such as mastering multiplication and division facts or increasing reading accuracy and fluency, will take many months, if not the entire year, and will require numerous practice and assessment items. Planning for reusable or digital resources rather than piles of consumables will save time and money. For example, reusable laminated practice sheets with white board markers or practice apps (if digital devices are available) will save on consumables. Station rotations can allow for independent, group, or pair practice on recursive standards with ease if they are stocked with aligned reusable digital and physical resources.

At times, even individual assessment questions may address more than one standard, such as this example from the New York State Department of Education's EngageNY (n.d.) mathematics curriculum, vetted for alignment with the Common Core State Standards. According to the key, this question addresses three third-grade Operations and Algebraic Thinking standards:

> Mrs. Tran plants 2 rows of 5 carrots in her garden.
>
> a. Draw an array that represents Mrs. Tran's carrots. Use an X to show each carrot.

b. Mrs. Tran adds 3 more rows of 5 carrots to her garden.

- Use circles to show her new carrots on the array in Part (a).

- Fill in the blanks below to show how she added the five rows.

  _____ fives + _____ fives = _____ fives

- Write a sentence to explain your thinking.

c. Find the total number of carrots Mrs. Tran planted.

d. Write a multiplication sentence to describe the array representing the total number of carrots Mrs. Tran planted. (EngageNY, n.d.)

Even with support documentation about which questions align with which standards, the teacher would still need to parse the aspects of each question that align with each listed standard. In *The New Art and Science of Classroom Assessment*, Marzano and colleagues (2019) stated that it is better to avoid tagging multiple standards for an assessment task because it makes it more difficult to determine precisely what students know and do not know. When teachers develop assessment items that address multiple standards, they often find that proving proficiency on specific skills is difficult, so the practice is not helpful. This does not assist the teachers in understanding what a student knows and is able to do in relation to the standards, nor does it assist students in tracking their learning progress. However, teachers who have less autonomy may find that they must continue using assessment items (like the preceding example) that do not have the ideal one standard, one assessment item alignment.

Educators must also consider the complexity level of assessment items compared with the standards. Does the assessment provide a body of evidence that would signify a student's mastery of all the skills and knowledge encompassed within the standard or standards? Often, end-of-chapter reviews and worksheets might include some lower-level content that covers only the basic expectations of a standard—the simpler skills, knowledge, and vocabulary that serve as an entry point or stepping-stone to the standard. These items are not rigorous enough to act as proof of mastery of the standard itself. Even so, teachers should not discard these items but should instead utilize them to prove understanding of the lower-level content expectations, which gives the teacher and student information about the student's current level of mastery in the learning process. The student may not have mastered the standard, but what *does* he or she know? When students and teachers can see what level of the content has been achieved, it is much easier for teachers to target the instruction and learning focus to what students truly need, as well as to celebrate levels of growth and success.

In addition to knowing the state or provincial expectations for standards, teachers should examine any district-level assessments for alignment with standards, especially noting if there are any gaps in the district expectations compared with curriculum resources. At times, district-level assessments have additional requirements or specific focus areas where students may need support in order to be successful. Assessment content should not come as a surprise to students, and in order to get accurate information on student achievement, the learning expectations, instruction, and assessment should all align.

This work of looking at standards and finding or developing aligned assessments is, of course, ideally done as a team, but for those teachers who are working in isolation, the very act of deeply understanding the standards and looking critically at assessment items will better the teachers' capacity. We have found during our years working within PCBE that any time spent delving into standards is time well spent. As educators develop a clearer understanding of the expectations of the standards, they can more easily transfer that clarity to their students, which in turn increases the student's ability to engage more deeply in their own learning process. For example, students who clearly understand the expectations of the standards will be able to suggest ways they might prove their mastery; these student-created assessment opportunities are meaningful ways that students can build strong agency within their learning.

Identifying Opportunities for Flexible Scheduling

Flexible scheduling within tightly structured programs or prescribed curriculum is challenging but possible. The pace aspect of the four Ps is one of the most difficult to address effectively, especially within an age-based classroom. That being said, even the most structured programs do allow for some flexibility of pacing to ensure that more students succeed, so teachers should identify areas where there is wiggle room, be it an extra two-day window of review and reteaching before a unit ends or daily flexibility within the instructional or practice components.

Most curriculum programs have at least twenty minutes of direct instruction, often followed by a session where students work through problems, examples, or text independently, with partners, or in groups. This is when additional direct instruction and guided practice for both the pedagogy and practice parts of the four Ps can occur for students needing additional challenge or support. Many programs also offer digital support materials. This makes personalization easier than ever before and allows for more one-on-one support throughout the learning process.

For educators with more autonomy to group and instruct students as they wish within their classrooms, expanded opportunities for flexibility would be available, allowing students to follow more individualized learner pathways. These pathways, when adopted by a school or district, allow flexibility within learning while meeting graduation requirements (Glossary of Education Reform, 2013). Since we are focusing here on implementation within individual classrooms, though, student pathways would allow students to have voice and choice in different areas of their learning (that is, within the four Ps), such as the method and mode of instruction, assessment, practice, and pace, as well as cultural and physical aspects such as behavioral goal setting and flexible seating choices.

Identifying Student Needs

As mentioned in chapter 1, within every age-based classroom, there will be students who can successfully follow the prescribed pace of the program, and there will be students who cannot. In fact, according to The Nation's Report Card (2019), in most U.S. schools, the students who cannot master content at the prescribed pace outnumber those who can. As table 6.1 shows, a majority of students are not proficient on grade-level standards in all core content areas.

Table 6.1: Proficiency Ranges for Mathematics and Reading Among U.S. Fourth-, Eighth-, and Twelfth-Grade Students in 2019

SUBJECT AREA	PERCENTAGE OF U.S. FOURTH GRADERS WHO SCORED PROFICIENT OR HIGHER	PERCENTAGE OF U.S. EIGHTH GRADERS WHO SCORED PROFICIENT OR HIGHER	PERCENTAGE OF U.S. TWELFTH GRADERS WHO SCORED PROFICIENT OR HIGHER
Mathematics	40	33	36
Reading	34	32	36
Writing	27	26	25
Science	37	33	21
Social Studies	Civics: 26 Geography: 20 U.S. History: 26	Civics: 23 Geography: 24 U.S. History: 23	Civics: 23 Geography: 19 U.S. History: 23

Source: National Center for Education Statistics, 2019.

Since age-based classrooms resources are geared toward grade-level content, most students will be behind the pace, with ever-widening gaps in their skills and knowledge. Obviously, this poses massive challenges to teachers and students and is a main argument for implementing PCBE. However, an individual classroom teacher working in isolation, regardless of level of autonomy, should first focus on determining exactly what each student knows and where the gaps lie.

To identify students' individual learning needs, educators would go through the same process that schools went through in the Establishing Student Data Based on Comprehensive Assessments section of chapter 2 (page 34). Once the comprehensive assessments are created, educators would follow the second approach to data collection outlined in chapter 2, Collecting Data at the Start of the Year (page 44). Due to the time-consuming nature of this task, educators might choose to slowly phase in this data collection to make it more manageable for themselves early on. For example, an educator who is a generalist teacher might choose to focus on one content area first and then move into other content areas over time. An educator specializing in one specific content area, such as mathematics, may choose to focus on one specific period or class within their schedule and slowly phase in more classes. In schools where teachers may already have access to specific student standards-based data, they would just need to analyze this data to figure out student needs.

Since teachers are attempting to do this in isolation, there will be no shared structure in place where students would be having a common experience across classrooms, so it is also a good practice to help students understand *why* the assessment is important. If teachers do not explain to students the purpose of a task or of the learning, they will draw their own conclusions, often based on erroneous or incomplete information (Sinek, 2009). Students should know that the comprehensive assessment is not for a report card, grade, or score but to assist them and their teacher in understanding their entry point into this year's learning. Students should know that this is so the teacher can accurately understand what they know and make better informed decisions about how to instruct and support them this year.

Teachers might also devise an additional input system that students can use as they work through the assessment items. Students might use a color code, words, or symbols to convey additional information to the teacher such as confidence level in the particular content covered by the questions, or whether the item was familiar to the student or not, hence indicating what their previous experience level with the content might be. For example, students might code each question based on the following three-point scale: (1) totally unfamiliar, (2) familiar but can't fully solve or answer, and (3) familiar and high level of confidence. Simply getting an incorrect answer doesn't necessarily indicate why the student got it wrong. If a student self-reported high familiarity and confidence on a question but got it incorrect, that could indicate simple mistakes due to speed, which could lead to additional data gathering and perhaps a quick refresher rather than a deep instructional unit on the topic. Any time a teacher can instruct and support students in a more targeted, efficient way, the better the chances of filling student learning gaps and increasing achievement.

Preparing for Flexible Instruction

After gathering student data, a teacher can examine the daily schedule and look for time that is available for flexible instruction in a certain content area or within a specific period. Teachers required to follow a prescribed curriculum might identify chunks of five to twenty minutes that can be perfect for administering targeted minilessons for those who need below- or above-grade-level content, in addition to the at-grade-level instruction they receive during the regular content-area instructional time.

Teachers with more autonomy may choose to fully implement flexible learning pathways to allow students to move through the standards at a pace that works best for them, utilizing support resources to navigate their learning. There are many ways to create this type of structure in a classroom, but the following example illustrates a possible way to incorporate flexible grouping and pacing within a classroom spanning a wide range of academic needs, in this case a self-contained multi-age special education classroom.

As students enter the classroom, their first stop is a prominently displayed bulletin board showing each student's daily agenda in a numbered grid. For anonymity and ease of identification, students each have their own number. Students come up to the board in the morning, find their number, and look at the first square in their row. There is either a number that corresponds with an activity, a symbol signifying working one on one or in small group with one of the teachers, or a symbol for a digital application or program to access on a device. The grid provides a step-by-step breakdown of the entire school day, each activity and expectation from the minute they enter to when they pack up to leave.

Since there is such a wide range of learning needs within this classroom, no two students have the same exact schedule, but there might some common tasks. The numbered activities correspond to clear numbered totes of differing sizes organized neatly on shelves beside the agenda board. Student 1, a fourth-grade-aged boy, points to the next number on his agenda and takes the corresponding tote off the shelf. Inside is a math activity where he can create repeated patterns with manipulatives. On the outside of the tote is a camera icon and Student 1 explains that he would take a picture of his finished products with his device and share it digitally to his teacher to show what he had worked on during his practice time.

Students in this classroom use three-ring data binders to track their progress on their IEP goals, which connect to standards. Student 1 knows his IEP goals from memory and expresses a great deal of pride when showing his progress and artifacts he'd produced during the year to show what he knew. Even with a significant disability, both cognitively and in speech, Student 1 explains how all the parts of the structure and process work, including the 1–4 scoring scale utilized. "1 is I really needed help. 2 is I kind of needed help. 3 is I got it," he says. In order to explain a 4 he turns back to his data binder and flips to a mathematics test. "See, this one I got a 4 on. That's better!"

This classroom had incorporated flexibility within all content areas, which requires a lot of preparation of materials and early support for students to learn the processes and procedures in order to begin to take more leadership of their learning. As mentioned previously, due to the amount of work involved in creating aligned resources, establishing procedures, and building student agency, we recommend focusing on one content area or one period of the day to start. Some content areas are more conducive than others for this work. For example, mathematics is a good place to start, as many skills build on each other, are relatively easy to parse, and can be mastered in a shorter span of time. By contrast, broad skills like narrative writing or fluent reading of grade-level texts take months or years to develop. For educators who teach multiple sections of the same subject, some class periods may be more conducive to start. For example, there may be a class where a majority of students are already able to work independently, or there is a narrower range of learning needs, which means less preparation is necessary.

The classroom example described previously had all students working on their own individual pathway or plan. This is the most difficult to achieve as instruction will most often happen one on one with constant movement from student to student to support their learning. More often, teachers will be able to group students who share common needs together and create rotational opportunities for instruction, feedback, and assessment. As students are initially grouped for a given content area based on their learning data, these groups will undoubtedly fluctuate as instruction shifts from topic to topic. Too often, teachers will assume that a student who is struggling with one particular concept struggles in that content area in general. Regrouping as needed during the course of the academic year allows for differing strengths within content areas, such as geometry, numeration, or measurement in mathematics or biology or physics in science as well as across content areas. Similarly, pacing may be different for students within the same group within a specific strand of a content area. For example, within Measurement and Data (NGA & CCSSO, 2010b), a student may easily master telling time but struggle with measuring using a ruler. A student might be more skilled at comprehending nonfiction books as opposed to fiction, or vice versa. Thus, it is important to allow for pacing differences or regrouping as needed.

As the class addresses different units of study, the teacher can give more targeted preassessments that cover the specific standards within each unit to a greater degree than the comprehensive preassessment. The recent information and data on the learning that has occurred since the cumulative preassessment can allow for change and guide the targeted instructional groupings. The groupings may be as simple as At Pace, Below Pace, and Above Pace for the entire unit or can be more nuanced to focus on single standards of need. Educators must take caution, however, to avoid falling into the same problem of tracking students that is present within the traditional educational system—that is, giving an incomplete or lower set of standards-based expectations to some students while others have a more rigorous or complete set of standards-based expectations. Since teachers in isolation are working within age-based restrictions and without the ability to afford systemwide flexibility of time, they operate within the confines of the school calendar year. This means students will leave them at the end of the year and will move to the next grade level regardless of how much they have mastered (except for rare cases when the student repeats the entire grade level), with the below-paced students suffering the most. There are a few things educators can do to help ameliorate this situation, but there will always be issues due to the wide range of needs presented by age-based class groupings. Some potential moderating approaches might include:

- Prioritizing standards to decrease the amount of content to cover for the year, guaranteeing a narrower but critical set of standards to all students

- Preassessing at the beginning of each strand of content instruction to ensure the most updated data and regrouping potential

- Requesting to loop with students for multiyear instruction

- Layering content instruction or practice to allow lagging students additional opportunities over time to continue toward mastery of multiple standards simultaneously

- Individualized homework or resource opportunities to focus on most critical needs

- Leveraging extra time within or outside the school day (for example, study halls, lunch club, summer school, tutoring) to provide additional targeted support

Though the issues of age-based grouping may not be solved by any one approach, utilizing as many potential tools as possible and thinking creatively in a solution-focused way can help offer more flexibility and success for more students.

Educators might alternatively decide to give grade-level direct instruction to all students at the same time (sometimes referred to as "teacher pace") and then break the class into needs-based groups after everyone has had the shared minilesson. Those who are not ready for this grade-level content are getting exposure to what will be coming up for them in the future, those on pace will continue to practice what they've learned from the lesson, and those above pace get a refresher on past learning, for example. Other classrooms might also utilize student helpers or teacher-created digital lessons for students to get additional instruction or support when the teacher is not available, as in the following example, shared during a classroom visit and interview with a high school math student.

"I scan the QR code here," she says, pointing to the top of a paper she is using. "And it comes up with an Educreations video, and I watch the video and I copy down the notes on my paper while one of the teachers writes it on theirs," she adds, showing the paused teacher-led video and its correlation to the paper she is working on. "Then there's some examples I have to do with the teacher." She shows how she follows along, working through problems as the teacher talks it out on the video.

When asked what she would do if she didn't understand something, she says, "I would either ask someone who's on the same unit as me"—pointing to the standards-aligned unit trackers that span the top edge of the classroom wall, where students move their names according to what unit they're on—"or I would ask to meet with the teacher for a minilesson." She points to the teacher circulating throughout the class, giving support, check-ins, and minilessons to students in need. She turns to a sleeve in her folder and pulls out another paper. "I have a syllabus of what I work on in order. So for A, it's pages 128 and 129 and these examples. So that's where I practice and get extra examples. This is the work I do before the quiz to get ready."

She says she likes working at her own pace. When asked what she likes about it, she says, "I like that you don't have to stay where the teacher is . . . like, if you fall behind or you don't understand something, you can take extra time, or you can go ahead if you master it faster. You know when you're ready. Like, we have a syllabus, but we also have a rubric so before we take the quiz, after we've done the required work, we have to fill out the rubric about how we are doing on each of these things."

She pulls out and shows the rubric. (Figure 6.6 features a generic version of the unit rubric and monitoring chart.) In this case, she is working on geometry unit 2, which has to do with using parallel and perpendicular lines. Her rubric lists the individual skills of the unit down the left column and includes areas for her to self-assess these skills and areas for her teacher to provide feedback on these skills as well.

Students are able to:	Student Self-Assessment			Notes	Teacher Assessment		
	E	P	A		E	P	A

E = Emerging; P = Proficient; A = Advanced

Figure 6.6: Unit rubric and monitoring chart.

"So, like, this E means 'I need help.' We check it off, like, 'I need help on this.'" For the sake *of illustrating her point, she makes a light check in the E column next to one of the skills. She says P means "I can do this on my own" and makes a check in the P column next to another skill. Finally, she says A means "I can teach someone," and she makes a check in the A column next to another skill. "We do this before we take the quiz to be sure we're ready, and our teacher checks us too."*

No matter how a teacher decides to group students, there will be a great need for cultural, structural, and operational elements that support all students in their learning progress. Lacking these structures, norms, and resources, students will be less successful working with the teacher, with their peers, and independently. With this in mind, we suggest referring to ideas outlined in chapter 2 of *A Handbook for Personalized Competency-Based Education,* "How Will the Learning Environment Support Student Agency?" (Marzano et al., 2017, p. 37) for more in-depth examples that support the creation of cultural, structural, and operational needs that teachers should consider in fostering PCBE-style classrooms.

Some questions that educators might consider when thinking about cultural elements are:

- What behavioral norms will help us build the greatest amount of student agency?
- How can I involve students in goal setting and monitoring their 21st century, social, and emotional skills and how will I impart strategies to support their growth?
- What will I do to ensure that all students have support and avenues for developing leadership?
- What elements need to be in place for students to help build and monitor the class culture together?
- How will I ensure that our class culture supports the growth and dignity of all students?

These critical areas of culture building expand far beyond traditional areas of class rules and jobs. Knowing how important these "soft skills" are for future success, taking time to develop cultural elements, will not only assist students in the classroom, but in every area of their lives.

When thinking about structural considerations for a PCBE-style classroom, teachers might address the following questions.

- What physical room layout would best support multiple stations or groupings?
- Where might various-sized groupings meet for direct instruction?
- Where and how might I store a variety of standards-based resources for the greatest ease of access with the least disruption?
- Where might I incorporate student voice and choice into the physical environment?
- Do I support efficient transitions through mindful room layout?
- Where might I utilize alternative environments?

There are innumerable ways to design for teaching and learning, so finding a setup that works for a teacher's class will often involve a lot of trial, feedback, and adjustment. It is not a fixed decision but a dynamic one that responds to changes in student and teacher needs throughout the course of the year.

Within the classroom, the teacher should plan for a variety of spaces where he or she can meet with groups of different sizes, be it at a separate table area, at a group of desks, at a side counter, around the teacher's desk, or on the floor. During this planning and arranging process, keep in mind that when teachers are giving direct instruction or support to a select group of students, the remaining students in the class are working on their own collaborative or independent learning. This means that the resources students will need during these independent work times have to be available to them somewhere in the classroom.

Having a variety of standards-based resources at multiple levels and in multiple content areas can take up a lot of space, so the teacher should thoughtfully choose a structural system to manage these materials. Office materials such as file folders and binders can be helpful in managing paper resources, but often, students will need additional materials such as manipulatives, tools, art supplies, and technological resources in order to practice different skills or processes. Additionally, there may be center activities or games that they use collaboratively to practice standards, so the teacher should carefully think out the space itself and the materials to utilize within that space, and he or she should provide those materials in an organized and easy way for students to identify and manage.

Another consideration is digital support. In many classrooms with devices, online platforms can store many needed practice materials, coded and housed according to standards. Just as with physical resources, though, careful thought and planning must go into the organizational system that will best support student learning, independence, and transparency. A teacher planning for these independent avenues should consider developing some of these structures with students, framing questions with them to help them understand the ultimate goal of the work that they will be doing in order to better master content and processes. It's also important to set up clear norms about utilizing shared digital spaces such as digital classrooms where students can see and comment on each other's work or participate in online discussions or collaborative work. They will need to know how to access what they need with ease, as well as how to be supportive of each other with respectful feedback and accountable work norms. This takes time and energy to develop initially but is critical to later success and builds important habits that will continue to enhance students' learning and lives.

Lastly, teachers might think about these questions when considering the operational needs required of a PCBE classroom.

- What materials will students be working with during independent or collaborative time?
- What guidance will they need about how to utilize and care for the materials?
- What guidance will they need about working together effectively?
- What clarity might they need about the structure and transitions during this time?
- What support might they need if they get stuck?
- What support might they need if they finish early?

The goal is to create, ideally *with* the students, procedural transparency and efficiency; this means that students know what work to do independently and when and how to do it, and they are able to successfully navigate and monitor their learning.

In addition to standard operating procedures (SOPs), teachers working in isolation might develop a variety of materials that students can practice with, and they might create a system for how students will work and track their progress. This may include a choice board, center rotations, or tutorial videos or links for online support. All of this takes time and organization to build and deploy. For every station or online support, teachers will have to develop or identify materials that align with the standards that will be addressed. Every choice board, center game, screencast, or tracking matrix means time spent, so teachers might identify just a few places to delve more deeply into; this makes it a more reasonable effort. Over time, teachers can identify and develop additional resources and add them to their repertoire so they build a larger base of materials to choose from and expand their flexibility, which was the case for a media center specialist who explained her flexibly paced library this way:

Using Edmodo in my classroom, the students all have their own individual login, and from my view we'll see all of the classes. . . . When they log in, it looks much like social media, and that alone excites the students in that they have this special place to be sharing about things that we're working on. But each week I'm able to post to them, and I use TeacherTube to record my lessons from home and I do screen captures of whatever research project they'll be working on, and they can hear my voice. So, I upload the video and kind of give them a short description of what we'll be working on, and I upload multiple videos at a time so that the students who are ready to move on can do so.

So, they know when they log in, they come and see which week they're working on. They open that video and they listen to maybe an eight- or nine-minute video of me explaining the lesson for the day. I touch on the standards and expectations, and we go through the entire lesson through the video, and then they actually go to work and put that lesson into place. With my elementary students . . . they will follow their graphic organizer to the website it directs them to, in this case PebbleGo. So, after the video, they will go to PebbleGo, complete their research, and afterwards come back to Edmodo, and at the end of class, they are to leave an exit ticket communicating to me . . . about what they learned about that day, and they can also ask questions.

I felt before when we were doing whole group that my students who could move ahead and were understanding the concepts that I was explaining were frustrated. . . . And then the students who were feeling like they weren't getting it were feeling a little bit behind and were also acting out for that reason, and now in one class, I have kids working on different weeks' assignments. I used to have to spend time managing behaviors, and now I'm celebrating the kids' successes, answering questions, getting new students caught up to our processes, and troubleshooting computers. It's freed up a lot of time for more productive work sessions.

I would say that 35 percent [of students] were engaged in the way I did things before, and now 100 percent, 100 percent of the time, are engaged.

With our toughest classes with our highest level of behavior problems, there is just an amazing amount of work happening and learning happening, and I find that they're excited about it, and that's the best part of all. They *want* to be in there doing what we're working on. They're upset when class is over. (C. Gerrity, personal communication, October 29, 2015)

Similarly, consider the following example of a kindergarten teacher who created resources aligned to her standards and put them in kid-friendly terms to display, along with tracking sheets where her students could access whatever they needed during independent practice time.

"I'm working on high-frequency words." A kindergarten student holds up a paper with choices aligned to this particular skill. The paper has pictures of different activities with smiley faces underneath each picture. He explains that he can practice the words by doing these activities. When asked how he knows what to do, he points to the first picture, which says Word Cards on it, and points to a tub with the same picture on the side; the tub is full of the materials he will need to practice high-frequency words in this way. When asked how he will know when he should meet with his teacher, he says, "When I've done these three times, in three different ways." He points to the three smiley faces underneath each picture and shows that he has colored one of the smiley faces underneath one of the pictures, two under another, and will begin working on his third. He will practice three different ways three times each, choosing whichever ways he wants before meeting with his teacher. There is also a space on the paper left blank that gives him the opportunity to come up with and draw his own way of practicing. When asked how he'll let his teacher know he's ready, he shows the folder on the wall where he'll put his choice board paper to signal he's ready for his teacher to give him a formal check.

When asked what happens then, he points to charts on the wall with different learning goals, such as "I can count to 100" and the one he is holding, "I can read high-frequency words." There, students each color in their attempts at mastery and track their progress. When asked when he thinks he'll be done with this goal, he looks at the chart, which shows he has had several instances of mastery, colored green, and he says, "Tomorrow, maybe," and smiles.

The guidelines and examples shared in this chapter are not a wholesale plan for implementation but rather a frame of reference for individualized classrooms, each one unique depending on the teacher, the classroom, and the students. From year to year, and even from week to week, changes and tweaks to the system are happening, with no cookie-cutter model. This is the personalized aspect of PCBE. It's personalized for the students, of course, but teachers also each bring their own strengths, passion, and creativity to the process. Teachers must certainly guarantee the standards, aligned assessment, and progress monitoring, but what that looks like might vary so long as teachers achieve the desired end—student growth along a transparent continuum of learning.

Summary

There are a variety of circumstances that teachers wishing to implement PCBE within their classrooms might find themselves in as they begin the implementation process. Depending on the amount of autonomy they have, teachers can implement different levels of flexibility within their classroom schedules. If they are working within their school's prescribed parameters in terms of pacing guides or programs, they might start by identifying their state or province standards, coding their program resources, and aligning their assessments with the individual standards. They should then identify opportunities for flexible scheduling and determine what the students know by giving standards-based preassessments. From there, they can identify segments of time within the schedule to give targeted instruction based on student needs. With greater autonomy, teachers may implement greater levels of flexible pacing within their classrooms. After teachers identify students' individual needs through cumulative preassessments, instructional groups provide the structure to fill learning gaps for students needing additional below-grade-level standards and to create opportunities for those needing above-grade-level standards.

No matter the degree of flexible scheduling, teachers can develop student agency by offering students voice, choice, and transparency to help build classroom structures, monitor progress, and develop a collaborative culture. There is no single way to build a PCBE classroom, but finding methods that address key PCBE components and involve the students in the process will help everyone grow together.

Epilogue

An effective personalized competency-based education system is a collection of elements that come together to create a comprehensive environment that addresses all aspects of student learning, with the specific learning needs of the student in relation to the standards acting as the focal point on which decision are made. These elements include an analytical view of academic content, the application of student agency, a new conception of instruction and measurement, schedules based on students' learning needs, and standards-based reporting for effective feedback to parents and students. As we have tried to illustrate, PCBE scheduling does not occur in isolation; rather, this process builds off the other elements within the PCBE system. Critically, this book assumes that readers' schools already have the other elements of PCBE in place or will have them in place before they address scheduling.

The goal of this book is to introduce processes and procedures that schools can employ when developing a PCBE schedule. All this information is designed to create a more holistic understanding of the PCBE scheduling process. This process forces schools that are transitioning to PCBE to question or rethink many traditional education norms, such as teacher certifications and student placement within classes. As Richard A. DeLorenzo, Wendy J. Battino, Rick M. Schreiber, and Barbara Gaddy Carrio (2009) stated in their book *Delivering on the Promise: The Education Revolution*, "Most efforts to improve the education system have failed because what was considered possible was limited by our shared, unquestioned assumptions and beliefs—our shared education paradigm" (p. 14). We need to question those paradigms that may be outdated or not serving students. We have to restructure many traditional scheduling systems to incorporate more of these PCBE components.

From this book, we hope readers take away an understanding of the importance of accurate student data and the processes for creating various schedules. When it comes to student data, averaged grades and broad test results are not sufficient to implement the PCBE scheduling process. Schools need to identify grade-level data and specific standards data for each student within the system before they can create an effective schedule. We explored two types of schedules—horizontal and vertical—in detail, but the processes described in this book are meant to be modified and adjusted to fit the needs of a specific school. The shift from age-based classes to need-based classes incorporates many factors that are unique to each school or district.

Share this information with your school or district, adapt it, and combine it with what is happening on site. Start out small when creating your first PCBE schedule by focusing on just one content area. Create the PCBE schedule for mathematics or ELA, and then design the rest of the schedule in a more traditional manner if need be. This incremental approach allows you to start working on the new procedures without creating huge tidal waves of change throughout the school. Work out the kinks when developing the schedule for the one content area. When the proper amount of student data is available and procedures are set, move to the next content area in the schedule.

With all the possible variations in creating a PCBE schedule, it is important to keep the end goal in mind. The point of creating a PCBE schedule is to develop a system that groups students within classes based on their learning needs. Both the students and the teachers benefit from this process because the range of information that each class covers focuses on the students' needs, which, in turn, creates a more sustainable teaching environment. The PCBE scheduling process is a learning experience—don't let the need for perfection stop you from trying.

Appendix

Example PCBE Schedules

A school's master schedule is often a complex, extensive document, and it can be difficult to imagine what a complete schoolwide PCBE schedule would look like. This appendix contains several example schedules drawn from real schools that have successfully implemented PCBE and the associated need-based scheduling practices.

Horizontal Schedule

Here is an example of a horizontal schedule from Benson Middle School in Benson, North Carolina. Figure A.1 (page 126) shows each teacher's class assignment during each period; figure A.2 (page 128) displays the school bell schedule. This schedule is designed to provide as many opportunities as possible to teach an interdisciplinary English language arts and social studies class (shown in the schedule as ELA/SS) within each class period. This is a good example of how the horizontal scheduling process needs to be slightly modified to adapt to real-life situations, such as the number of certified teachers, lunch, and electives. In each period there are at least ten to eleven ELA/SS classes for students to be placed based on their learning needs. Note that the bell schedule includes a combined power block and lunch period. While students are not at lunch, the power block focuses on individual learning needs. Students are assigned to different teachers to address specific learning gaps and thus improve performance in their regular classes.

Grades 5–6

Block 1	ELA/SS Teacher 1 (25)	Science Teacher 6 (25)	ELA/SS Teacher 4 (23)	Math Teacher 5 (25)	ELA/SS Teacher 3 (23)	ELA/SS Teacher 7 (27)	Science Teacher 2 (29)	ELA/SS Teacher 8 (28)	Math Teacher 9 (29)
Block 2	5th Electives	5th Electives	5th Electives	5th Electives	5th Electives	6th Electives	6th Electives	6th Electives	Science Teacher 10 (29)
Block 3	ELA/SS Teacher 1 (25)	Math Teacher 5 (25)	ELA/SS Teacher 4 (23)	Science Teacher 6 (25)	ELA/SS Teacher 3 (23)	Math Teacher 6 (28)	ELA/SS Teacher 8 (28)	ELA/SS Teacher 8 (28)	6th Electives
Block 4	Science Teacher 2 (25)	ELA/SS Teacher 7 (25)	Science Teacher 10 (23)	ELA/SS Teacher 4 (25)	Math Teacher 9 (23)	Science Teacher 5 (28)	Science Teacher 5 (27)	ELA/SS Teacher 5 (27)	ELA/SS Teacher 1 (29)
Block 5	Math Teacher 9 (25)	ELA/SS Teacher 7 (25)	Math Teacher 10 (23)	ELA/SS Teacher 4 (25)	Science Teacher 2 (23)	ELA/SS Teacher 8 (28)	Math Teacher 6 (27)	Math Teacher 6 (27)	ELA/SS Teacher 1 (29)

Grades 7–8

Block 1	ELA/SS Teacher 11 (29)	Science Teacher 14 (22)	ELA/SS Teacher 12 (19)	Math Teacher 13 (20)	Math Teacher 35 (25)	ELA/SS Teacher 16 (19)	Science Teacher 17 (24)	ELA/SS Teacher 19 (19)	Science Teacher 20 (25)	ELA/SS Teacher 21 (20)	Math Teacher 18 (28)
Block 2	ELA/SS Teacher 11 (29)	Math Teacher 13 (22)	ELA/SS Teacher 12 (19)	Science Teacher 14 (23)	Science Teacher 15 (24)	ELA/SS Teacher 16 (19)	Math 1 Teacher 35 (17)	ELA/SS Teacher 19 (21)	Math Teacher 20 (16)	ELA/SS Teacher 21 (20)	Science Teacher 17 (28)
Block 3	Science Teacher 14 (29)	ELA/SS Teacher 15 (22)	Math Teacher 13 (19)	ELA/SS Teacher 12 (21)	ELA/SS Teacher 11 (23)	Science Teacher 17 (18)	ELA/SS Teacher 16 (26)	Math Teacher 20 (23)	ELA/SS Teacher 19 (25)	Math Teacher 18 (20)	ELA/SS Teacher 21 (26)
Block 4	7th Electives	7th Electives	7th Electives	7th Electives	7th Electives	Math 1 Teacher 18 (18)	ELA/SS Teacher 16 (26)	Science Teacher 17 (21)	ELA/SS Teacher 19 (25)	Science Teacher 20 (20)	ELA/SS Teacher 21 (26)
Block 5	Math Teacher 13 (29)	ELA/SS Teacher 15 (22)	Science Teacher 14 (19)	ELA/SS Teacher 12 (21)	ELA/SS Teacher 11 (24)	8th Electives	8th Electives	8th Electives	8th Electives	8th Electives	8th Electives

Block 1	Planning	Planning	Planning	Planning	Planning	Planning	Planning	Planning
Block 2	5th Grade Art Teacher 36	5th Grade Music Teacher 37	5th Grade Physical Education Teacher 38	5th Grade Media Center Teacher 39	5th Grade Spanish I Teacher 40	5th Grade Band Teacher 41	5th Grade CTE Technology Teacher 42	5th Grade CTE Agriculture Teacher 43
Block 3	6th Grade Art Teacher 36	6th Grade Music Teacher 37	6th Grade Physical Education Teacher 38	6th Grade Media –Center Teacher 39	6th Grade Introduction to Spanish I Teacher 40	6th Grade Band Teacher 41	6th Grade CTE Technology Teacher 42	6th Grade CTE Agriculture Teacher 43
Block 4	7th Grade Art Teacher 36	7th Grade Music Teacher 37	7th Grade Physical Education Teacher 38	7th Grade Media Center Teacher 39	7th Grade English Second Language I Teacher 40	7th Grade Band Teacher 41	7th Grade CTE Technology Teacher 42	7th Grade CTE Agriculture Teacher 43
Block 5	8th Grade Art Teacher 36	8th Grade Music Teacher 37	8th Grade Physical Education Teacher 38	8th Grade Media Center Teacher 39	8th Grade English Second Language I Teacher 40	8th Grade Band Teacher 41	8th Grade CTE Technology Teacher 42	8th Grade CTE Agriculture Teacher 43

Key:

ELA/SS = combined class content using social studies topics to drive ELA learning

Teacher 1 = Teacher name

25 = number of students per class

Source: © 2020 by Benson Middle School. Used with permission.

Figure A.1: Benson Middle School master schedule.

Time	Minutes	Block	Fifth Grade	Sixth Grade	Seventh Grade	Eighth Grade	Electives
7:50–8:20	30	Breakfast					
8:20–8:25	5	Homeroom					
8:25–9:30	65	Block 1	Core Content Class	Core Content Class	Core Content Class	Core Content Class	Planning
9:32–10:37	65	Block 2	Planning	Core Content Class	Core Content Class	Core Content Class	Fifth Grade
10:39–11:44	65	Block 3	Core Content Class	Planning	Core Content Class	Core Content Class	Sixth Grade
	POWER Block						
11:45–12:08	23	1st Lunch; Fifth-Grade Students (B Side of Cafeteria)					
11:55–12:18	23	2nd Lunch; Seventh-Grade Tutorials (A Side of Cafeteria)					
12:12–12:35	23	3rd Lunch; Enrichment Students from Seventh/Eighth-Grade Hall (B Side of Cafeteria)					
12:22–12:45	23	4th Lunch; Enrichment Students from Elective Wing and Fifth/Sixth-Grade Hall (A Side of Cafeteria)					
12:39–1:02	23	5th Lunch; Eighth-Grade Tutorials/100 Hall (B Side of Cafeteria)					
12:49–1:12	23	6th Lunch; Sixth-Grade Tutorials/Intramurals (A Side of Cafeteria)					
1:14–2:18	65	Block 4	Core Content Class	Core Content Class	Planning	Core Content Class	Seventh Grade
2:20–3:25	65	Block 5	Core Content Class	Core Content Class	Core Content Class	Planning	Eighth Grade
3:25–3:30	5	Prepare For Dismissal					

Source: © 2020 by Benson Middle School. Used with permission.

Figure A.2: Benson Middle School bell schedule.

Vertical Schedules

Here, we present examples of vertical PCBE schedules from three schools in Colorado's Westminster Public School District: (1) Westminster High School, (2) Hodgkins Leadership Academy, and (3) Sunset Ridge Elementary School. We have had a long-running relationship with Westminster Public School District, working with them to help develop their personalized competency-based educational system.

Westminster High School

Westminster Public School District in Westminster, Colorado, has been working with scheduling in a PCBE system since 2009, and it has put the concepts of alignment, flexibility, and student interests into action. Figure A.3 (page 130) presents the actual schedule that Westminster High School used during the 2019–2020 school year. The schedule includes all the school's subject areas with a total of 114 teachers covering all those subject areas. Figure A.4 (page 140) displays the bell schedules.

CAREER AND TECHNICAL EDUCATION	BLOCK 1	BLOCK 2	BLOCK 3	BLOCK 4	BLOCK 5	BLOCK 6	BLOCK 7
Teacher 1	Education Exploration (1st Semester) / Child Development (2nd Semester)	Plan	Early Childhood Education	Education Exploration (1st Semester) / Child Development (2nd Semester)	Education Exploration (1st Semester) / Child Development (2nd Semester)	Education Exploration (1st Semester) / Child Development (2nd Semester)	Early Childhood Education
Teacher 2	Intro to Urban Agriculture (1st Semester) / Agricultural Mechanics (2nd Semester)	Intro to Urban Agriculture (1st Semester) / Agricultural Mechanics (2nd Semester)	Greenhouse Management	Floral Design	Pre-Veterinary	Animal Science	Plan
Teacher 3	Aviation History (JROTC)	Aviation History (JROTC)	Aviation History (JROTC)	Aviation History (JROTC)	Plan	Aviation History (JROTC)	Aviation History (JROTC)
Teacher 4	Capstone	Plan	Technology Essentials	Technology Essentials	Technology Essentials	Engineering Design and Development	Engineering Design and Development
Teacher 5	Personal Computer Maintenance	Cybersecurity	Plan	Video-Game Design	Video-Game Design	Technology Essentials	Technology Essentials
Teacher 6	Construction 1	Construction 1	Construction 1	Construction 1	Plan	Construction 2	Construction 2
Teacher 7	Agricultural Fabrication	Agricultural Fabrication	Intro to Urban Agriculture (1st Semester) / Agricultural Mechanics (2nd Semester)	Intro to Urban Agriculture (1st Semester) / Agricultural Mechanics (2nd Semester)	Energy Systems	Agricultural Mechanics	Plan
Teacher 8	Principles of Marketing	Principles of Marketing	Business Applications	Principles of Business	Principles of Business	Plan	Principles of Business
Teacher 9	Intro to Health Occupations	Intro to Health Occupations	Intro to Health Occupations	Intro to Health Occupations	Plan	Health Occupations Practicum	
Teacher 10	Technology Essentials	Technology Essentials	Technology Essentials	Plan	Technology Essentials	Technology Essentials	Technology Essentials
Teacher 11	ProStart 1	Plan	Plan	Culinary Arts	Culinary Arts	Catering	Catering

	BLOCK 1	BLOCK 2	BLOCK 3	BLOCK 4	BLOCK 5	BLOCK 6	BLOCK 7
Teacher 12	Aviation History / JROTC	Aviation History / JROTC	Aviation History / JROTC	Cadet Corps / JROTC	Plan	Cadet Corps / JROTC	Cadet Corps / JROTC
Teacher 13	Video Cinema Arts Live Broadcast	Video Cinema Arts Live Broadcast	Video Cinema Arts Live Broadcast	Video Cinema Arts 3—Documentary	Plan	Advanced Video Cinema Arts	Technology Essentials
CULTURALLY AND LINGUISTICALLY DIVERSE (CLD)							
Teacher 14	CLD Intervention and Monitoring	CLD Intervention and Monitoring	CLD Intervention and Monitoring	Plan	Language Acquisition 1	Language Acquisition 1	Language Acquisition 2
Teacher 15	Language Acquisition 2	Language Acquisition 2 and 3	Language Acquisition 2 and 3	Plan	Admin	Language Acquisition 2	Language Acquisition 2
Teacher 16	Admin	Plan	Language Acquisition 1 (SpEd)	Newcomer English 1	Newcomer English 1	Newcomer English 2	Newcomer English 2
Teacher 17	Language Acquisition 1	Plan	Admin	Language Acquisition 1	Language Acquisition 1	Language Acquisition 1	Language Acquisition 1
Teacher 18	Admin	Plan	Language Acquisition 2	Language Acquisition 2	Language Acquisition 2	Language Acquisition 2	ELA 1 (Sheltered)
Teacher 19	Language Acquisition 1	Language Acquisition 1	Language Acquisition 1	Admin	Plan	Language Acquisition 1	Language Acquisition 1
Teacher 20	Extended Literacy—Newcomers	Extended Literacy	Language Acquisition and CLD Co-Teach	Language Acquisition and CLD Co-Teach	Language Acquisition and CLD Co-Teach	Language Acquisition and CLD Co-Teach	Plan
Teacher 21	AVID 9-10	Language Acquisition (AVID 12)	Plan	Admin	Language Acquisition 1	Language Acquisition 1	Language Acquisition 1
LANGUAGE ARTS							
Teacher 22	Plan	ELA 1	ELA 3+	ELA 3+ Co-Teach	ELA 3+	ELA 3+ Co-Teach	ELA 3+
Teacher 23	ELA 2-R	ELA 2-R	ELA 2-R	Plan	Humanities—ELA 2	Humanities—ELA 2	ELA 2-R
Teacher 24	IB World Literature—Higher Level 2	IB World Literature—HL 2	Plan	GT Release Period	ELA 2	ELA 2	ELA 2

Figure A.3: Westminster High School master schedule.

continued →

LANGUAGE ARTS	BLOCK 1	BLOCK 2	BLOCK 3	BLOCK 4	BLOCK 5	BLOCK 6	BLOCK 7
Teacher 25	English Language Arts 3+	ELA 3+	AIM Sophomore Cohort—ELA 2	AVID 9-10	Plan	AIM Sophomore Cohort—ELA 2	ELA 3+
Teacher 26	ELA 3—Advanced Genre Studies	Instructional Coaching	Instructional Coaching	Instructional Coaching	Instructional Coaching	Instructional Coaching	Instructional Coaching
Teacher 27	ELA 1-R	ELA 3-R	ELA 1-R	ELA 1-R	ELA 1-R	ELA 1-R	Plan
Teacher 28	AVID 9-10	Plan	Humanities—Literature	Humanities—Literature	AP (Advanced Placement) English Literature and Composition	AP English Literature and Composition	AP English Literature and Composition
Teacher 29	ELA 4	ELA 4	AIM Freshman Cohort—ELA Concepts	AIM Freshman Cohort—ELA Concepts	ELA Concepts	ELA Concepts	Plan
Teacher 30	IB World Literature—HL1	IB World Literature—HL1	IB World Literature—HL1	IB World Literature—HL1	ELA 1	Plan	Yearbook 1 and 2
Teacher 31	ELA 1	ELA 1	Humanities—Literature	Humanities—Literature	ELA 1 Co-Teach	ELA 1 Co-Teach	Plan
Teacher 32	ELA 2	ELA 2	ELA 1	Plan	ELA 1	ELA 2	ELA 2
Teacher 33	ELA 2 Co-Teach	ELA 2 Co-Teach	ELA 2 Co-Teach	ELA 2	ELA 1	Plan	ELA 1
Teacher 34	ELA Concepts (1st Semester) / ELA 1 Co-Teach (2nd Semester)	ELA Concepts (1st Semester) / ELA 1 Co-Teach (2nd Semester)	ELA Concepts (1st Semester) / ELA 1 Co-Teach (2nd Semester)	Plan	ELA Concepts (1st Semester) / ELA 1 Co-Teach (2nd Semester)	ELA 4	ELA 4
Teacher 35	ELA 1	Newspaper 1 and 2	ELA 1	Plan	IB World Literature—HL1	IB World Literature—HL1	IB World Literature—HL1

MATHEMATICS	BLOCK 1	BLOCK 2	BLOCK 3	BLOCK 4	BLOCK 5	BLOCK 6	BLOCK 7
Teacher 36	Algebra and Geometry 1—Ninth Grade	Algebra and Geometry 1—Ninth Grade	Algebra and Geometry 1—Ninth Grade	Algebra and Geometry 1—Tenth Grade	Plan	Algebra and Geometry 1—Ninth Grade	Algebra and Geometry 1—Ninth Grade
Teacher 37	Algebra and Geometry 3	Algebra and Geometry 3	Algebra and Geometry 3	Algebra and Geometry 3	Plan	IB Math Studies—SL1	IB Math Studies—SL1
Teacher 38	Algebra and Geometry 2—Eleventh Grade	Algebra and Geometry 2	Algebra and Geometry 2	Algebra and Geometry 2	Plan	IB Math—SL1	IB Math—SL1

Teacher							
Teacher 39	Plan	Algebra and Geometry 1	Algebra and Geometry 1	Algebra and Geometry 1 Co-Teach	Algebra and Geometry 1	Algebra and Geometry 2	Algebra and Geometry 2
Teacher 40	Algebra and Geometry Concepts	Algebra and Geometry Concepts	AIM Freshman Cohort—Algebra and Geometry Concepts	Algebra and Geometry Concepts	Algebra and Geometry Concepts	AIM Freshman Cohort—Algebra and Geometry Concepts	Plan
Teacher 41	Algebra and Geometry 3	Algebra and Geometry 3	Algebra and Geometry 3	Algebra and Geometry 3	Algebra and Geometry 3	Plan	IB Math—SL2
Teacher 42	Algebra and Geometry 2—Eleventh and Twelfth Grade	AVID 9-10	Consumer Business	Plan	Consumer Business	Consumer Business	AVID 9-10
Teacher 43	Algebra and Geometry 1—Tenth-Grade Co-Teach	Algebra and Geometry 1—Tenth-Grade Co-Teach	Algebra and Geometry 1—Tenth-Grade Co-Teach	Algebra and Geometry 1—Ninth Grade	Algebra and Geometry 1—Ninth and Tenth Grade	Plan	AP Statistics
Teacher 44	Curriculum Development	Plan	Algebra and Geometry Concepts Co-Teach	Algebra and Geometry Concepts Co-Teach	Mathematics Support and Co-Teach	Algebra/ Geometry Concepts Co-Teach	Mathematics Support and Co-Teach
Teacher 45	Algebra/ Geometry 2	Algebra/ Geometry 2	Algebra/ Geometry 2	Plan	Algebra/ Geometry 2	Algebra/ Geometry 2	Algebra/ Geometry 2
Teacher 46	Construction Geometry	Instructional Coaching	Instructional Coaching	Instructional Coaching	Plan	Instructional Coaching	IB Math Studies—SL2
Teacher 47	College Algebra	Algebra/ Geometry 1	College Algebra	College Algebra	Plan	Algebra/ Geometry 1	Algebra/ Geometry 1
Teacher 48	Algebra and Geometry 1	Algebra and Geometry 1	Plan	PLTW—Engineering Architecture	PLTW—Engineering Architecture	Computer Science	Computer Science
Teacher 49	Plan	Algebra and Geometry 2 Co-Teach	AIM Sophomore Cohort—Algebra 1	AIM Sophomore Cohort—Algebra 1	Algebra and Geometry 2 Co-Teach	Algebra and Geometry 2	Algebra and Geometry 2 Co-Teach

continued →

PERFORMING ARTS	BLOCK 1	BLOCK 2	BLOCK 3	BLOCK 4	BLOCK 5	BLOCK 6	BLOCK 7
Teacher 50	Guitar	Guitar	Piano	Piano	Plan	Los Lobos	Piano
Teacher 51	Theater / Adaptive Theater	Theater (Advanced Theater)	Theater	Theater 2 / Theater (Advanced Theater)	Stagecraft	Advanced Stagecraft	Plan
Teacher 52	Westy Singers	Essence	Swing Set	Chamber Choir	Raging Harmonies	Plan	Sirens
Teacher 53	Plan	Jazz Laboratory	Jazz Ensemble	Wind Ensemble	Symphonic Band	Plan	Concert Band
Teacher 54	Plan	Camerata Orchestra	Orchestra	Concert Orchestra	Sinfonia Orchestra	Mariachi Ensemble	Mariachi

PHYSICAL EDUCATION	BLOCK 1	BLOCK 2	BLOCK 3	BLOCK 4	BLOCK 5	BLOCK 6	BLOCK 7
Teacher 55	Weights	Weights	Weights	Adaptive Education	Plan	Weights	Athletic Team Fitness
Teacher 56	Physical Education	Physical Education	Physical Education	Health	Health	Plan	Physical Education (1st Semester) Athletic Team Fitness (2nd Semester)
Teacher 57	Physical Education	Health	Physical Education	Weights	Weights	Physical Education	Plan
Teacher 58	Physical Education	Physical Education	Health	Plan	Physical Education	Bowling	Athletic Team Fitness (1st Semester) Physical Education (2nd Semester)
Teacher 59	Health	Physical Education (1st Semester) Plan (2nd Semester)	Bowling	Physical Education	Physical Education	Physical Education	Plan (1st Semester) Athletic Team Fitness (2nd Semester)
Teacher 60							Athletic Team Fitness

PROJECT LEAD THE WAY (PLTW)	BLOCK 1	BLOCK 2	BLOCK 3	BLOCK 4	BLOCK 5	BLOCK 6	BLOCK 7
Teacher 61	PLTW—Biomedical Science	PLTW—Biomedical Science	PLTW—Biomedical Science	PLTW—Medical Interventions	PLTW—Medical Interventions	Plan	PLTW—Medical Interventions
Teacher 62	PLTW—Human Body Systems	PLTW—Human Body Systems	PLTW—Human Body Systems	PLTW—Human Body Systems	Plan	PLTW—Human Body Systems	PLTW—Biomedical Science
Teacher 63	PLTW—Bio Innovation	PLTW—Bio Innovation	PLTW—Bio Innovation	PLTW—Biomedical Science	PLTW—Biomedical Science	PLTW—Biomedical Science	Plan
SCIENCE	BLOCK 1	BLOCK 2	BLOCK 3	BLOCK 4	BLOCK 5	BLOCK 6	BLOCK 7
Teacher 64	Chemistry	Chemistry	Chemistry	Chemistry	AIM Sophomore Cohort—Chemistry	AIM Sophomore Cohort—Chemistry	Plan
Teacher 65	Chemistry-R	Chemistry-R	Chemistry-R	Plan	Chemistry-R	Chemistry-R	Biology
Teacher 66	Plan	Science and Mathematics Intervention	Chemistry-R—Seniors (D101)	Chemistry-R—Seniors (D101)	Science and Mathematics Intervention	Science and Mathematics Intervention	Physics-R
Teacher 67	AP Biology	AP Biology	Plan	AVID	Biology	IB Biology—HL2	Biology
Teacher 68	PLTW—Introduction to Engineering Design	PLTW—Introduction to Engineering Design	PLTW—Introduction to Engineering Design	PLTW—Introduction to Engineering Design	PLTW—Introduction to Engineering Design	IB Physics—SL	Plan
Teacher 69	Chemistry	Chemistry	Chemistry	AIM Ninth—Science Concepts	AIM Ninth—Science Concepts	Science Concepts	Plan
Teacher 70	IB Biology—HL1	Plan	IB Biology—HL1	IB Biology—HL1	IB Biology—HL1	IB Biology—HL1	IB Biology—HL1
Teacher 71	Chemistry	Chemistry	Chemistry	AP Environment	PLTW—Environmental Sustainability	Plan	Chemistry
Teacher 72	Physics-R	Physics-R	Physics	Physics	Plan	Science Concepts	Science Concepts
Teacher 73	Physics	Physics	Physics	Plan	Physics	Physics	Physics
Teacher 74	Physics	Physics	Biology Co-Teach	Biology	Plan	Physics	Physics
Teacher 75	Instructional Coaching	Instructional Coaching	Biology	Instructional Coaching	Plan	Physics	Physics
Teacher 76	Physics	Physics	Physics	IB Physics—SL2	Physics	Plan	Physics

continued ↓

SCIENCE	BLOCK 1	BLOCK 2	BLOCK 3	BLOCK 4	BLOCK 5	BLOCK 6	BLOCK 7
Teacher 77	Plan	Physics-R (1st Semester) Chemistry-R (2nd Semester)	Physics-R	Physics-R	Physics-R	Biology	Biology
Teacher 78	Biology	Biology	Chemistry	Chemistry	Chemistry	Chemistry	Plan

SOCIAL STUDIES	BLOCK 1	BLOCK 2	BLOCK 3	BLOCK 4	BLOCK 5	BLOCK 6	BLOCK 7
Teacher 79	Civics (1st Semester) Economics (2nd Semester)	Civics (1st Semester) Economics (2nd Semester)	Civics (1st Semester) Economics (2nd Semester)	Plan	Humanities—Social Studies 2 (Civics and Economics)	Humanities—Social Studies 2 (Civics and Economics)	Civics (1st Semester) Economics (2nd Semester)
Teacher 80	IB Psychology—SL	IB Psychology—SL	IB Psychology—SL	IB Psychology—SL	IB Psychology—SL	Plan	U.S. History-R
Teacher 81	Project-Based Learning Coaching	Project-Based Learning Coaching	IB Psychology—SL2	IB Psychology—SL2	Psychology (1st Semester) Sociology (2nd Semester)	Psychology (1st Semester) Sociology (2nd Semester)	Plan
Teacher 82	World History (1st Semester) Geography (2nd Semester)	Economics	World History (1st Semester) Geography (2nd Semester)	World History (1st Semester) Geography (2nd Semester)	World History (1st Semester) Geography (2nd Semester)	Plan	Economics
Teacher 83	Psychology (1st Semester) Sociology (2nd Semester)	Psychology (1st Semester) Sociology (2nd Semester)	U.S. History	Plan	U.S. History	U.S. History	U.S. History
Teacher 84	Alternative to Suspension—Re-Engage	Alternative to Suspension—Re-Engage	Alternative to Suspension—Re-Engage	AIM Sophomore Cohort—Civics/Economics	AIM Sophomore Cohort—Civics and Economics	Plan	Psychology (1st Semester) Sociology (2nd Semester)
Teacher 85	IB History of the Americas—SL2	U.S. History-R	Civics (1st Semester) Economics (2nd Semester)	Civics (1st Semester) Economics (2nd Semester)	U.S. History-R	U.S. History-R	Plan

	BLOCK 1	BLOCK 2	BLOCK 3	BLOCK 4	BLOCK 5	BLOCK 6	BLOCK 7
Teacher 86	AVID 11-12	Plan	Humanities—Social Studies (U.S. History)	Humanities—Social Studies (U.S. History)	IB History of the Americas—SL1	AVID 11-12	AVID 11-12
Teacher 87	Civics (1st Semester) Economics (2nd Semester)	Civics (1st Semester) Economics (2nd Semester)	Civics (1st Semester) Economics (2nd Semester)	Civics (1st Semester) Economics (2nd Semester)	Plan	Civics (1st Semester) Economics (2nd Semester)	Athletic Team Fitness
Teacher 88	U.S. History	U.S. History	U.S. History	U.S. History	Plan	U.S. History	U.S. History
Teacher 89	U.S. History	U.S. History	Humanities—Social Studies (U.S. History)	Humanities—Social Studies (U.S. History)	U.S. History	U.S. History	Plan
Teacher 90	Plan	World History (1st Semester) Geography (2nd Semester)	World History (1st Semester) Geography (2nd Semester)	Civics (1st Semester) Economics (2nd Semester)	Civics (1st Semester) Economics (2nd Semester)	World History (1st Semester) Geography (2nd Semester)	World History-R (1st Semester) Civics (2nd Semester)
Teacher 91	Plan	Civics	U.S. History	Civics	AIM Freshman Cohort—U.S. History	AIM Freshman Cohort—U.S. History	Social Studies-R Co-Teach
STUDENT SERVICES							
Teacher 92	Plan	General Skills Math 2	General Skills Math 2	Plan	General Skills Math 1	General Skills Math 1	General Skills Math 1
Teacher 93	General Skills Literacy 1	Algebra and Geometry 1 Co-Teach	AIM Sophomore Cohort—Algebra 1	Algebra and Geometry 1 Co-Teach	Plan	Plan	General Skills Literacy 1
Teacher 94	ELA Concepts (1st Semester) ELA 1 (2nd Semester)	ELA Concepts (1st Semester) ELA 1 (2nd Semester)	ELA Concepts (1st Semester) ELA 1 (2nd Semester)	Plan	ELA 1	ELA 1	Plan
Teacher 95	Algebra and Geometry 1 Co-Teach	Algebra and Geometry 1 Co-Teach	Algebra and Geometry 1 Co-Teach	Plan	Plan	Credit Recovery	Credit Recovery
Teacher 96	General Skills Civics and Economics	Plan	General Skills Civics and Economics	General Skills Civics and Economics	Life Skills Social Studies	General Skills Civics and Economics	Plan
Teacher 97	ELA 2	ELA 2	ELA 2	ELA 3+	Plan	ELA 3+	Plan
Teacher 98	Plan	Life Skills Science	General Skills Earth Science	General Skills Earth Science	Life Skills Science	General Skills Earth Science	General Skills Earth Science

continued →

STUDENT SERVICES	BLOCK 1	BLOCK 2	BLOCK 3	BLOCK 4	BLOCK 5	BLOCK 6	BLOCK 7
Teacher 99		Plan	Algebra Concepts Co-Teach	Algebra Concepts Co-Teach	Algebra and Geometry 2 Co-Teach	Algebra and Geometry 2 Co-Teach	Algebra and Geometry 2 Co-Teach
Teacher 100	Plan	ASP Independent Living		Plan	ASP Literacy	ASP Math	ASP Science
Teacher 101	Life Skills Literacy	Life Skills Literacy	Plan	Life Skills Literacy	Plan	Independent Living	Independent Living
Teacher 102	General Skills Literacy 4	General Skills Literacy 3	Plan	General Skills Literacy 2	Plan	General Skills Literacy 2	General Skills Literacy 2
Teacher 103	Life Skills Math	Plan	Life Skills Math	Plan	Life Skills Math	Independent Living	

VISUAL ARTS	BLOCK 1	BLOCK 2	BLOCK 3	BLOCK 4	BLOCK 5	BLOCK 6	BLOCK 7
Teacher 104	Painting 1.2.3	2-D Art	IB Visual Art—SL2 and HL2	Plan	IB Visual Art—SL1 and HL1	2-D Art	2-D Art
Teacher 105	Adaptive Art (1st Semester) 2-D Art (2nd Semester)	Drawing 1.2.3	2-D Art	2-D Art	2-D Art	Plan	Drawing 1.2.3
Teacher 106	3-D Art	3-D Art	Jewelry 1.2.3	3-D Art	Sculpture 1.2.3	3-D Art	Plan
Teacher 107	Graphic Design and Interactive Media 1	Graphic Design and Interactive Media 1	Graphic Design and Interactive Media 1	Intro to Visual Communication (1st Semester) Adobe (2nd Semester)	Intro to Visual Communication (1st Semester) Adobe (2nd Semester)	Graphic Design and Interactive Media 2 and 3	

WORLD LANGUAGE	BLOCK 1	BLOCK 2	BLOCK 3	BLOCK 4	BLOCK 5	BLOCK 6	BLOCK 7
Teacher 108	Plan	IB Spanish A—Juniors	IB Spanish A—Juniors	AP Spanish Literature and Culture	IB Spanish A—Seniors	Spanish 3 and 4	Spanish 3
Teacher 109	Spanish 1	Spanish 1	Spanish 1	Spanish 1	IB Spanish—SL2	Spanish 1	Plan
Teacher 110		Plan	Chinese	Chinese	Chinese	Library	Library
Teacher 111	Spanish Language Arts 1	Spanish Language Arts 1	Spanish Language Arts 1	Plan	Spanish 2	Spanish 2	Spanish 2

	Block 1	Block 2	Block 3	Block 4	Block 5	Block 6	Block 7
Teacher 112	French 1	IB French—SL1 (1st Semester) / French 3 (2nd Semester)	French 1	French 1	IB French—SL2 (1st Semester) / French 4 (2nd Semester)	Plan	French 1
Teacher 113	French 1	French 1	French 2	Plan	French 1	French 2	French 2
YOUTH EMPOWERMENT SUPPORT SERVICES	BLOCK 1	BLOCK 2	BLOCK 3	BLOCK 4	BLOCK 5	BLOCK 6	BLOCK 7
Teacher 114	YESS	YESS	YESS	YESS	YESS	YESS	Plan

Source: © 2019 by Westminster Public Schools. Used with permission.

Key:

R—course sections designated for students who need more time to complete standards

GT—gifted and talented

AVID—Advance Via Individual Determination

PLTW—Project Lead The Way

2019–2020 Bell Schedule		
Monday/Tuesday/Friday	Wednesday	Thursday
Block 1 7:05–8:05	Block 1 7:05–8:28	Block 4 7:05–8:28
Block 2 8:10–9:03	Academic Enrichment 8:33–9:21	Academic Enrichment 8:33–9:25
Block 3 9:08–10:01	Block 2 9:26–10:49	Block 5 9:30–10:53
Block 4 10:06–10:59	Block 3* 10:54–12:55	Block 6* 10:58–12:57
Block 5* 11:04–12:29	*A Lunch 10:49–11:32 *B Lunch 12:17–12:55	Block 7 1:02–2:25
Block 6 12:34 – 1:27		*A Lunch 10:58–11:34 *B Lunch 12:21–12:57
Block 7 1:32–2:25		
*A Lunch 10:59–11:36 *B Lunch 11:57–12:34		

Late Start or Weather Delay Schedule		Assembly Schedule	
Block 1	9:05–9:41 a.m.	Block 1	7:05–7:47 a.m.
Block 2	9:46–10:22a.m.	Block 2	7:52–8:34 a.m.
Block 3	10:27–11:03 a.m.	Block 3	8:39–9:21 a.m.
Block 4	11:08–11:44 a.m.	Block 4	9:26–10:08 a.m.
Block 5	11:49 a.m.–1:03 p.m.	Block 5	10:13–10:55 a.m.
Block 6	1:08–1:44 p.m.	Block 6	11:00 a.m.–12:20 p.m.
Block 7	1:49–2:25 p.m.	Block 7	12:25–1:07 p.m.
Lunches are during Block 5 A Lunch: 11:49 a.m.–12:25 p.m. B Lunch: 12:30 p.m.–1:08 p.m.		Lunches are during Block 5 A Lunch: 11:00–11:40 a.m. B Lunch: 11:42 a.m.–12:20 p.m.	

Source: © 2019 by Westminster Public Schools. Used with permission.

Figure A.4: Westminster High School bell schedules.

Peter Rainey, the assistant principal and administrator responsible for developing this schedule, had this to say about creating a PCBE schedule:

An effective master schedule, developed in a horizontal or vertical approach, must be driven by the needs and desires of your students. A master schedule that results in meeting the aforementioned requires agile teachers, creative resource allocation, passionate leadership, and a never-ending process of Plan, Do, Check, Adjust.

Westminster High School's (WHS's) master schedule can best be described as fitting in a vertical-scheduling process. The constant exists that students need a variety of "entry and exit" points throughout the school year related to scheduled courses. Within WHS's' Competency-Based System, students are supported to matriculate through proficiencies or proficiency scales at a pace that best meets their mastery and learning capacity. Therefore, a primary value when constructing the master schedule is to align multiple courses within a content in a vertical structure to ensure students who are moving through the scales quickly can be provided a secondary course enrollment at the completion of a given content level.

A student who is quickly mastering the content of English language arts 1 (level 9) may need to be "rescheduled" in November, to the next content level, based on the individual needs of the student. To minimize the impact on the totality of the student schedule across the seven-period structure, WHS ensures levels 9–12 are placed in each period, to the greatest degree possible, allowing the student's easy movement. Additionally, WHS schedules courses that include the opportunity for off-schedule instruction, be it recovery or advancement. These courses are resourced with a smaller teacher-student ratio to maximize one-on-one and small-group instruction based on the individual matriculation of each individual student. This, too, is an opportunity for a student to continue to progress and/or receive targeted intervention, in an off-schedule way related to a traditional semester schedule setup.

Overall, the key approach to the construction of an effective [competency-based education] master schedule is maximizing the points at which students are able to enter and exit a scheduled learning opportunity. Moreover, there cannot be one content area valued more than another to ensure maximum variability of placement, and movement, and always operate on the needs and passions of learners. (personal communication, February 25, 2020)

Hodgkins Leadership Academy

At Hodgkins Leadership Academy, a preK–6 school also part of Westminster Public Schools, principal Amber Swieckowski had this to say about planning for, developing, and adjusting her school's schedule based on student need:

> When developing our master schedule, we took into consideration the varying needs of our students. To do this, we had to look at our interventionists' schedules differently. Instead of all interventionists pulling at the same time, culturally and linguistically diverse (CLD) interventionists pull students from a specific pod (team of three teachers) and then when that forty-five-minute block is over, Title and Special Education interventionists pull students for their intervention. The "why" behind this schedule change was to allow those students who are second language learners who are ready for reading instruction the ability to see both interventionists or specialists. This also allows those students with Individual Education Plans (IEPs) to be seen by a variety of specialists for a variety of Tier 2 intervention. (personal communication, February 28, 2020)

Figure A.5 shows the schedule for each of the school's twenty-four generalist teachers.

Sunset Ridge Elementary School

At Sunset Ridge, a preK–5 school within Westminster Public Schools, principal Roger Vadeen described the decisions he and his team reached in devising their master block schedule as well as their interventionist and special-area schedules (see figures A.6–A.9, pages 145–147):

> At Sunset Ridge, we initially group our students by instructional level for literacy. Literacy groups are determined by an analysis of student data including: Empower; DIBELS; Scantron; and teacher anecdotal notes. We do not want more than two instructional levels in any one class. We also do not want more than two grade levels in any one class. With that said, grade-level outliers are the exception and we may have a class that has a younger or older student who is best suited for that class. For our intermediate students, we regroup students during the lunch hour for math groups. We have created "measured pace" and "accelerated pace" groups for levels 3–5. For example, the level 4 "measured pace" math group will be working on level 4 performance scales and learning topics but at a pace that allows for more opportunities for concrete and pictorial experiences. Fewer students will be placed in the measured pace group, and Title I math support is also provided to students during their math measured pace group.

Teacher 1	Mathematics	Literacy	Lunch	Literacy	CLD Flex	Title Flex	Literacy	Elective	Science / Social Studies
Teacher 2	Mathematics	Literacy	Lunch	Literacy	CLD Flex	Title Flex	Literacy	Elective	Science / Social Studies
Teacher 3	Mathematics	Literacy	Lunch	Literacy	CLD Flex	Title Flex	Literacy	Elective	Science / Social Studies
Teacher 4	Mathematics	Literacy	Lunch	Literacy	CLD Flex	Title Flex	Literacy	Science / Social Studies	Elective
Teacher 5	Title Flex	CLD Flex	Literacy	Literacy	Lunch	Literacy	Science / Social Studies	Elective	Mathematics
Teacher 6	Title Flex	CLD Flex	Literacy	Literacy	Lunch	Literacy	Science / Social Studies	Elective	Mathematics
Teacher 7	Title Flex	CLD Flex	Literacy	Literacy	Lunch	Literacy	Mathematics	Science / Social Studies	Elective
Teacher 8	CLD Flex	Title Flex	Literacy	Lunch	Literacy	Science / Social Studies	Elective	Mathematics	Mathematics
Teacher 9	CLD Flex	Title Flex	Literacy	Lunch	Literacy	Science / Social Studies	Elective	Mathematics	Mathematics
Teacher 10	CLD Flex	Title Flex	Literacy	Lunch	Literacy	Science / Social Studies	Elective	Mathematics	Mathematics
Teacher 11	Literacy	Elective	Science / Social Studies	Lunch	Literacy	Mathematics	CLD Flex	Mathematics	Mathematics
Teacher 12	Literacy	Elective	Science / Social Studies	Lunch	Literacy	Mathematics	CLD Flex	Mathematics	Mathematics
Teacher 13	Literacy	Elective	Science / Social Studies	Lunch	Literacy	Mathematics	CLD Flex	Mathematics	Mathematics
Teacher 14	Literacy	Title Flex	CLD Flex	Elective	Lunch	Literacy	Science / Social Studies	Mathematics	
Teacher 15	Literacy	Title Flex	CLD Flex	Elective	Lunch	Literacy	Science / Social Studies	Mathematics	
Teacher 16	Literacy	Title Flex	CLD Flex	Elective	Lunch	Literacy	Science / Social Studies	Mathematics	
Teacher 17	Mathematics	Literacy	CLD Flex	Lunch	Literacy	Science / Social Studies	Literacy	Title Flex	Literacy
Teacher 18	Mathematics	Literacy	CLD Flex	Lunch	Literacy	Science / Social Studies	Literacy	Title Flex	Literacy
Teacher 19	Mathematics	Literacy	CLD Flex	Lunch	Literacy	Science / Social Studies	Literacy	Title Flex	Literacy
Teacher 20	Mathematics	Literacy	CLD Flex	Literacy	Lunch	Science / Social Studies	Literacy	Elective	
Teacher 21	Mathematics	Elective	CLD Flex	Mathematics	Title Flex	Literacy	Science / Social Studies	Lunch	Mathematics	Science / Social Studies
Teacher 22	Literacy	Elective	CLD Flex	Literacy	Literacy	Science / Social Studies	Mathematics	Lunch	Mathematics	Science / Social Studies
Teacher 23		Literacy	Lunch		Science / Social Studies	Literacy	Elective	Mathematics	
Teacher 24		Literacy	Lunch		Science / Social Studies	Literacy	Elective	Mathematics	

Source: © 2019 by Westminster Public Schools.

Figure A.5: Hodgkins Leadership Academy vertical schedule.

By doing this, we strategically provide more adult supports and explicitly create more opportunities for individual support for our students struggling with math understandings. The accelerated pace group will have larger numbers and will be challenged with additional math application opportunities and complex problem solving. Math groups will be multi-aged, and typically no more than two grade levels in the group. Math groups are created between two [professional learning community] teams, meaning two teachers create math groups from their two literacy groups. Students are placed in accelerated or measured pace groups through an analysis of a preassessment given at the beginning of a unit study. As needed, students move from one group to the next based on student need. Students transition back to their literacy groups at the end of the day to retrieve backpacks and coats and prepare for dismissal. (personal communication, February 28, 2020)

The Sunset Ridge Elementary School master schedule (figure A.6) is based on the different levels of learning that are needed for the entire student body. It identifies which general education teachers are teaching each level and the times throughout the day for each period. Literacy is the anchor content area and is used to create the levels of learning. Literacy and mathematics are categorized as either morning or afternoon to give flexibility to the teachers in covering those content areas. In some cases science and social studies are embedded in the literacy block and do not have a specific time of day for instruction.

The Sunset Ridge Elementary School master block schedule for Title I and special education (SpEd) intervention and specials (figure A.7, page 146) shows two different aspects of their schedule. The Title I and SpEd interventionists have specific times of the day to be in certain locations, indicated in the first two columns. The specials teachers (physical education, music, and art) have a much more general schedule indicating a certain number of minutes that are devoted to instruction, lunch, recess supervision, and classroom support. An additional schedule is created to clarify specific locations and times for each specialist.

KINDERGARTEN LEVELS	TEACHERS	LITERACY BLOCK	MATHEMATICS BLOCK	SPECIALS BLOCK	LUNCH	SCIENCE AND SOCIAL STUDIES BLOCK	RECESS	CLD BLOCK
Level 0	Teacher 1	Afternoon	Morning	1:30–2:15 p.m.	11:25 a.m.–12:00 p.m.	11:00–11:25 a.m.	9:55–10:10 a.m.	2:15–3:00 p.m.
	Teacher 2	Afternoon	Morning	1:30–2:15 p.m.	11:25 a.m.–12:00 p.m.	11:00–11:25 a.m.	9:55–10:10 a.m.	2:15–3:00 p.m.
PRIMARY LEVELS	**TEACHERS**	**LITERACY BLOCK**	**MATHEMATICS BLOCK**	**SPECIALS BLOCK**	**LUNCH**	**SCIENCE AND SOCIAL STUDIES BLOCK**	**RECESS**	**CLD BLOCK**
Levels 0 and 1	Teacher 3	Afternoon	Morning	2:20–3:05 p.m.	11:00–11:35 a.m.	Embedded in Literacy	9:55–10:10 a.m.	12:30–1:15 p.m.
Level 1	Teacher 4	Afternoon	Morning	1:30–2:15 p.m.	11:00–11:35 a.m.	Embedded in Literacy	9:55–10:10 a.m.	12:30–1:15 p.m.
Levels 1 and 2	Teacher 5	Afternoon	Morning	2:20–3:05 p.m.	11:10–11:45 a.m.	Embedded in Literacy	9:55–10:10 a.m.	1:20–2:05 p.m.
Level 2	Teacher 6	Afternoon	Morning	2:20–3:05 p.m.	11:10–11:45 a.m.	Embedded in Literacy	9:55–10:10 a.m.	1:20–2:05 p.m.
INTERMEDIATE LEVELS	**TEACHERS**	**LITERACY BLOCK**	**MATHEMATICS BLOCK**	**SPECIALS BLOCK**	**LUNCH**	**SCIENCE AND SOCIAL STUDIES BLOCK**	**RECESS**	**CLD BLOCK**
Level 3	Teacher 7	Morning	Afternoon	10:00–10:45 a.m.	11:45 a.m.–12:20 p.m.	Embedded in Literacy	1:45–2:00 p.m.	9:15–10:00 a.m.
	Teacher 8	Morning	Afternoon	10:00–10:45 a.m.	11:45 a.m.–12:20 p.m.	Embedded in Literacy	1:45–2:00 p.m.	9:15–10:00 a.m.
Level 4	Teacher 9	Morning	Afternoon	9:10–9:55	11:55 a.m.–12:30 p.m.	Embedded in Literacy—Social Studies Focus	1:45–2:00 p.m.	8:20–9:05 a.m.
	Teacher 10	Morning	Afternoon	9:10–9:55	11:55 a.m.–12:30 p.m.	Embedded in Literacy—Social Studies Focus	1:45–2:00 p.m.	8:20–9:05 a.m.
Level 5	Teacher 11	Morning	Afternoon	8:20–9:05 a.m.	12:05–12:40 p.m.	Embedded in Literacy—Science Focus	1:45–2:00 p.m.	10:15–11:00 a.m.
	Teacher 12	Morning	Afternoon	8:20–9:05 a.m.	12:05–12:40 p.m.	Embedded in Literacy—Science Focus	1:45–2:00 p.m.	10:15–11:00 a.m.

Source: © 2019 by Westminster Public Schools. Used with permission.

Figure A.6: Sunset Ridge Elementary School master block schedule.

TITLE I or SpEd	PE	MUSIC	ART
8:20–9:10 a.m. (50 minutes)	PE day 1 (150 minutes)	Music day 1 (250 minutes)	Art day 1 (250 minutes)
9:10–10:00 a.m. (50 minutes)	PE day 2 (250 minutes)	Music day 2 (250 minutes)	Art day 2 (150 minutes)
10:00–10:50 a.m. (50 minutes)	PE day 3 (250 minutes)	Music day 3 (150 minutes)	Art day 3 (250 minutes)
12:15–1:05 p.m. (50 minutes)	Lunch and recess coverage	Lunch and recess coverage	Lunch and recess coverage
1:05–1:55 p.m. (50 minutes)			
2:20–3:05 p.m. (45 minutes)			
Progress monitoring (25 minutes per day)			
Total = 320 minutes	Total = 220 minutes (average over three days)	Total = 220 minutes (average over three days)	Total = 220 minutes (average over three days)
	100 minutes per day providing support in classrooms	100 minutes per day providing support in classrooms	100 minutes per day providing support in classrooms

Source: © 2019 by Westminster Public Schools. Used with permission.

Figure A.7: Sunset Ridge Elementary School master block schedule for Title I and SpEd intervention and specials.

Figure A.8 displays the master bell schedule for Sunset Ridge Elementary School.

PERIODS	TIME
Breakfast in the classroom	8:05–8:20 a.m.
Block 1	8:20–9:15 a.m.
Block 2	9:15–10:00 a.m.
Block 3	10:00–10:50 a.m.
Specials or Planning	10:50–11:40 a.m.
Lunch Break	11:40 a.m.–12:15 p.m.
Block 4	12:15–1:05 p.m.
Block 5	1:05–1:55 p.m.
Progress Monitoring	1:55–2:15 p.m.
Block 6	2:15–3:05 p.m.

Source: © 2019 by Westminster Public Schools. Used with permission.

Figure A.8: Sunset Ridge Elementary School general master bell schedule.

Figure A.9 outlines the daily CLD teacher schedule, which corresponds with the final column on the master schedule (figure A.6, page 145).

PERIODS	TIME	LEVELS ADDRESSED
Breakfast in the classroom	8:05–8:20 a.m.	
Block 1	8:20–9:15 a.m.	Level 4
Block 2	9:15–10:00 a.m.	Level 3
Block 3	10:15–11:00 a.m.	Level 5
Planning and Progress Monitoring	11:00–11:55 a.m.	
Lunch Break	11:55 a.m.–12:30 p.m.	
Block 4	12:30–1:15 p.m.	Levels 0 and 1
Block 5	1:20–2:05 p.m.	Levels 1 and 2
Block 6	2:15–3:00 p.m.	Level 0

Source: © 2019 by Westminster Public Schools. Used with permission.

Figure A.9: Sunset Ridge Elementary School CLD blocks.

References and Resources

Blatchford, P., Bassett, P., & Brown, P. (2011). Examining the effect of class size on classroom engagement and teacher-pupil interaction: Differences in relation to pupil prior attainment and primary vs. secondary schools. *Learning and Instruction, 21*(6), 715–730. Accessed at http://citeseerx.ist.psu.edu/viewdoc/download?doi=10.1.1.469.8472&rep=rep1&type=pdf on September 10, 2019.

Brown, P., Roediger, H., III, & McDaniel, M. (2014). *Make it stick: The science of successful learning.* Cambridge, MA: Harvard University Press.

Colorado Department of Education. (2019, August 9). *Spring 2019 CMAS data and results.* Accessed at http://www.cde.state.co.us/assessment/cmas-dataandresults-2019 on July 4, 2020.

Conner, D. (2012, August 15). *The real story of the burning platform* [Blog post]. Accessed at www .connerpartners.com/frameworks-and-processes/the-real-story-of-the-burning-platform on June 10, 2019.

DeLorenzo, R. A., Battino, W. J., Schreiber, R. M., & Carrio, B. G. (2009). *Delivering on the promise: The education revolution.* Bloomington, IN: Solution Tree Press.

Duckworth, A. (2020). *Grit scale.* Accessed at https://angeladuckworth.com/grit-scale/ on July 10, 2020.

DuFour, R., DuFour, R., & Eaker, R. (2007, September 13). *The case for common formative assessments* [Blog post]. Accessed at www.allthingsplc.info/blog/view/17/the-case-for-common -formative-assessments on July 28, 2019.

EngageNY. (n.d). *Grade 3 mathematics module 1.* Accessed at https://www.engageny.org/resource /grade-3-mathematics-module-1/file/112411 on July 3, 2020.

Firmender, J. M., Reis, S. M., & Sweeny, S. M. (2012). Reading comprehension and fluency levels ranges across diverse classrooms: The need for differentiated reading instruction and content. *Gifted Child Quarterly, 57*(1), 3–14. Accessed at http://uwm.kbd.on-rev.com/summer15/july30 /docs/Firmender_2013.pdf on September 26, 2019.

Fullan, M. (2001). *Leading in a culture of change.* San Francisco: Jossey-Bass.

Galoppin, L. (2011). The giant misunderstanding on burning platforms. *Reply online magazine for organizational change practitioners.* Accessed at http://www.reply-mc.com/2011/01/17/the-giant -misunderstanding-on-burning-platforms/ on July 8, 2020.

Glossary of Educational Reform. (2013). *Learning pathway.* Accessed at https://www.edglossary.org /learning-pathway/ on July 10, 2020.

Hattie, J. (2018). *Hattie effect size list—256 influences related to achievement.* Accessed at https:// visible-learning.org/hattie-ranking-influences-effect-sizes-learning-achievement/ on September 8, 2018.

Heflebower, T., Hoegh, J. K., & Warrick, P. (2014). *A school leader's guide to standards-based grading.* Bloomington, IN: Marzano Resources.

Maine Department of Education. (n.d.). *Standards and instruction: Visual and performing arts— Complete visual and performing arts standards.* Augusta, ME: Author. Accessed at www.maine .gov/doe/learning/content/arts/standards on July 23, 2019.

Marzano, R. J. (2003). *What works in schools: Translating research into action.* Alexandria, VA: Association for Supervision and Curriculum Development.

Marzano, R. J. (2010). *Formative assessment and standards-based grading.* Bloomington, IN: Marzano Resources.

Marzano, R. J., Norford, J. S., Finn, M., & Finn, D., III. (2017). *A handbook for personalized competency-based education.* Bloomington, IN: Marzano Resources.

Marzano, R. J., Norford, J. S., & Ruyle, M. (2019). *The new art and science of classroom assessment.* Bloomington, IN: Solution Tree Press.

Marzano, R. J., Waters, T., & McNulty, B. A. (2005). *School leadership that works: From research to results.* Alexandria, VA: Association for Supervision and Curriculum Development.

Mayer, R. E. (2009). *Multimedia learning.* New York: Cambridge University Press.

Mindset Works. (2017). *Mindset assessments.* Accessed at https://www.mindsetworks.com/assess/ on July 10, 2020.

National Center for Education Statistics. (n.d.a). *Digest of education statistics: 2017.* Accessed at https://nces.ed.gov/programs/digest/d17/ch_2.asp on October 22, 2019.

National Center for Education Statistics. (n.d.b). *Fast facts: Teacher trends.* Accessed at https://nces .ed.gov/fastfacts/display.asp?id=28 on October 22, 2019.

National Education Association. (n.d.). *Research spotlight on project-based learning.* Accessed at http://www.nea.org/tools/16963.htm on July 3, 2020.

National Governors Association Center for Best Practices & Council of Chief State School Officers. (2010a). *Common Core State Standards for English language arts and literacy in history/social studies, science, and technical subjects.* Washington, DC: Authors. Accessed at www.corestandards .org/assets/CCSSI_ELA%20Standards.pdf on September 29, 2019.

National Governors Association Center for Best Practices & Council of Chief State School Officers. (2010b). *Common Core State Standards for mathematics.* Washington, DC: Authors. Accessed at www.corestandards.org/assets/CCSSI_Math%20Standards.pdf on May 20, 2019.

The Nation's Report Card. (2019). *How did U. S. students perform on the most recent assessments?* Washington, DC: Authors. Accessed at https://www.nationsreportcard.gov/ on June 29, 2020.

Office of Special Education Programs. (n.d.). *School accommodations and modifications.* Accessed at https://osepideasthatwork.org/node/116 on August 15, 2019.

Pink, D. H. (2009). *Drive: The surprising truth about what motivates us.* New York: Riverhead Books.

Public School Review. (n.d.). *Average public school student size.* Accessed at www.publicschoolreview .com/average-school-size-stats/national-data on October 22, 2019.

Rettig, M. D. (1999). The effects of block scheduling. *School Administrator, 56*(3). Accessed at www.aasa.org/SchoolAdministratorArticle.aspx?id=14852 on November 12, 2019.

Sanders, W. L., & Rivers, J. C. (1996, November). *Cumulative and residual effects of teachers on future student academic achievement.* Knoxville: University of Tennessee Value-Added Research and Assessment Center. Accessed at www.beteronderwijsnederland.nl/files/cumulative% 20and%20residual%20effects%20of%20teachers.pdf on September 10, 2019.

Sievertsen, H. H., Gino, F., & Piovesan, M. (2016). Cognitive fatigue influences students' performance on standardized tests. *Proceedings of the National Academy of Sciences, 113*(10), 2621–2624. Accessed at www.pnas.org/content/113/10/2621 on September 3, 2019.

Sinek, S. (2009). *Start with why: How great leaders inspire everyone to take action.* New York: Portfolio.

Singh, A., Uijtdewilligen, L., Twisk, J. W. R., van Mechelen, W., & Chinapaw, M. J. M. (2012). Physical activity and performance at school: A systematic review of the literature including a methodological quality assessment. *Archives of Pediatrics and Adolescent Medicine, 166*(1), 49–55. Accessed at https://jamanetwork.com/journals/jamapediatrics/fullarticle/1107683 on May 16, 2019.

Solution Tree. (2009, October 9). *Solution Tree: Dr. Marzano on second-order change* [Video file]. Accessed at www.youtube.com/watch?v=tqRWXv6ZTLk on May 6, 2020.

South Carolina Department of Education. (2017). *South Carolina college- and career-ready standards for visual arts proficiency.* Columbia: Author. Accessed at https://ed.sc.gov/scdoe/assets/File /instruction/standards/Visual%20Arts/Visual_Arts_Design_and_Media_Arts_Standards.pdf on July 23, 2019.

Tennessee Department of Education Division of Data and Research. (2016, March). *Equitable access to highly effective teachers for Tennessee students.* Nashville: Tennessee Department of Education. Accessed at www.tn.gov/content/dam/tn/education/reports/equitable_access_web.pdf on September 10, 2019.

U.S. Department of Education. (2019, August 30). *A guide to the Individualized Education Program.* Accessed at www2.ed.gov/parents/needs/speced/iepguide/index.html#writing on May 16, 2019.

Westminster Public Schools. (2013). *District 50 graduation rate up, dropout rate down.* Accessed at https://www.westminsterpublicschools.org/Page/4853 on July 4, 2020.

Westminster Public Schools. (2019a). *Graduation rates continue to climb as dropout rates decline.* Accessed at https://www.westminsterpublicschools.org/site/Default.aspx?PageType=3&Domain ID=1&PageID=1&ViewID=6446ee88-d30c-497e-9316-3f8874b3e108&FlexDataID=20732 on July 4, 2020.

Westminster Public Schools. (2019b). *Test results show steady improvement for WPS students.* Accessed at https://www.westminsterpublicschools.org/site/Default.aspx?PageType=3&DomainID =1&PageID=1&ViewID=6446ee88-d30c-497e-9316-3f8874b3e108&FlexDataID=17595 on July 4, 2020.

Index

A Handbook for Personalized Competency-Based Education
Robert J. Marzano, Jennifer S. Norford, Michelle Finn, and Douglas Finn III
Ensure all students master content by designing and implementing a personalized competency-based education (PCBE) system. Explore examples of how to use proficiency scales, standard operating procedures, behavior rubrics, personal tracking matrices, and other tools to aid in instruction and assessment.
BKL037

Vision and Action
Charles M. Reigeluth and Jennifer R. Karnopp
Transform teaching and learning with personalized competency-based education (PCBE). With the support of this comprehensive guide, discover how to define your vision of PCBE and then learn how to fully realize this vision by implementing the system across your school or district.
BKL040

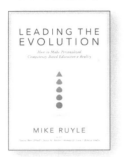

Leading the Evolution
Mike Ruyle with Tamera Weir O'Neill, Jeanie M. Iberlin, Michael D. Evans, and Rebecca Midles
Take action to evolve the existing model of schooling into one that is more innovative, relevant, and effective. Leading the Evolution introduces a three-pronged approach to driving substantive change—called the evolutionary triad—that connects transformational leadership, student engagement, and teacher optimism around personalized competency-based education.
BKL042

Beyond Reform
Lindsay Unified School District
Learn how Lindsay Unified School District took action to improve student learning by shifting from a traditional time-based education system to a learner-centered performance-based system. By adopting and tailoring Lindsay Unified's instructional model, you and your team can embark on your own district's transformation.
BKL036

Personalized Learning in a PLC at Work®
Timothy Stuart, Sascha Heckmann, Mike Mattos, and Austin Buffum
Rely on this resource to help you build a highly effective learning-progressive school. You will learn how to engage students in personalized learning experiences and empower them to take ownership of the four critical questions of the PLC at Work® process.
BKF703

MARZANO Resources

Visit MarzanoResources.com or call 888.849.0851 to order.

GLOBAL PD

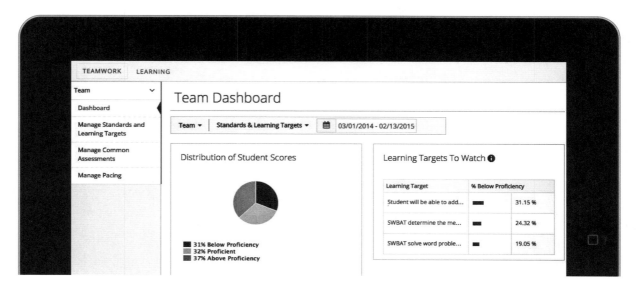

The **Power to Improve**
Is in Your Hands

Global PD gives educators focused and goals-oriented training from top experts. You can rely on this innovative online tool to improve instruction in every classroom.

- Get unlimited, on-demand access to guided video and book content from top Solution Tree authors.

- Improve practices with personalized virtual coaching from PLC-certified trainers.

- Customize learning based on skill level and time commitments.

▶ **REQUEST A FREE DEMO TODAY**
SolutionTree.com/GlobalPD

 Solution Tree